By Kelsey Ale

about me.

Kelsey Ale is a certified Nutritional Therapy Practitioner and Paleo chef/baker living in Santa Monica, California. She discovered her passion for healthy cooking and desserts over 15 years ago. Shortly after, she started running the juice bar at her local health food store where her love for holistic health began to grow. But she still faced severe health challenges of her own. After discovering how the Paleo diet and other natural lifestyle adjustments helped her heal her own body and recover from illness, Kelsey became fully committed to showing the world how to use delicious food to lose weight, increase mental clarity and energy, and achieve vibrant health.

"Follow me on Instagram and Facebook @thekelseyale to get natural health tips, down-to-earth nutrition advice that works, yummy recipes, and more!"

— Kelsey, www.KelseyAle.com

contents.

Brownies

Cake

Cheesecakes

Pies

Cookies

Ice cream

brownies

CARAMEL BROWNIES

🍴 SERVES: 12-16   🕐 PREP: 20 MINS   🕐 COOK: 50 MINS

INGREDIENTS:

Caramel Layer

- ½ cup ghee
- ½ cup coconut sugar
- ¼ cup full fat coconut milk
- 1 tsp vanilla
- Pinch of sea salt
- 3 tbsp tahini

Brownie Layer

- ½ cup coconut oil
- 4 oz unsweetened baking chocolate
- 1 cup almond flour
- ¾ cup coconut sugar
- 3 eggs
- 1 tbsp vanilla extract

METHOD:

Prepare caramel first:

1. Preheat oven to 350°F. Combine all ingredients in a small saucepan and heat until the ghee is melted, stirring occasionally to combine.
2. When the mixture is smooth and completely combined, continue to stir to allow caramel to thicken, 3-5 minutes.
3. Remove caramel from heat and allow it to cool while you prepare the brownie batter.

Prepare the brownie batter:

1. In a small saucepan, heat the coconut oil and chocolate over low heat until melted. Remove pan from heat, stir to combine ingredients, and set aside.
2. In a medium bowl combine the almond flour and coconut sugar and stir to incorporate.
3. Add the melted chocolate and oil and combine.
4. Add eggs and vanilla and mix to completely combine.

To assemble the brownies:

1. Line an 8x8x2-inch baking dish with parchment paper.
1. Pour ⅔ of the brownie batter into the lined 8x8x2 baking dish and bake for 15 minutes.
2. Remove the dish from the oven and add the caramel layer.
3. Using a spoon, dollop the remaining brownie batter over the caramel layer, and swirl to incorporate.
4. Return the dish to the oven and finish baking for 25 more minutes.

To serve:

Allow the brownies to cool fully in the pan before removing and slicing. These brownies can be made the day before and chilled in the fridge overnight before slicing and serving.

MINT BROWNIES

MAKES 12-16 SERVINGS • **PREP: 55 MINS** • **COOK: 30 MINS**

INGREDIENTS:

Brownie Layer

- ½ cup coconut oil
- 4 oz unsweetened baking chocolate
- ¾ cup coconut sugar
- 1 tbsp vanilla extract
- 3 eggs
- 1 cup almond flour
- ¼ tsp salt (optional)

Mint Frosting

- 2 tbsp honey
- 2 tbsp maple syrup
- ¼ cup arrowroot starch
- ½ cup palm shortening
- 10 drops liquid chlorophyll, for color
- 2 tsp peppermint extract

Chocolate Layer

- ½ cup melted ghee or coconut oil
- 2 oz unsweetened baking chocolate
- ¼ cup honey

METHOD:

Make the brownie layer first:

1. Preheat oven to 350°F. Line an 8x8x2-inch baking dish with parchment paper and set aside.
2. In a small saucepan, heat coconut oil and chocolate over low heat until melted. Remove from heat, stir, and set aside.
3. In a large bowl, mix sugar, vanilla, and eggs until smooth. Add almond flour and optional salt. Stir to blend. Add the coconut oil-chocolate mixture and mix until completely combined.
4. Pour into lined baking dish and spread batter to make an even layer. Bake for 25-30 minutes, until a toothpick inserted into the middle comes out mostly clean. Set aside to cool completely.

For the frosting layer:

1. In a medium bowl, whisk honey and maple syrup with arrowroot starch until a smooth paste is formed.
2. Add the shortening and whip with electric mixer until fully combined.
3. Add chlorophyll and peppermint extract and continue whipping until just combined. Spread the frosting over the cooled brownies all the way to the edges of the pan. Place in freezer to set, about 30 minutes.

Chocolate ganache:

1. Combine oil and chocolate in the bowl of a double boiler and heat over medium until the ingredients are melted.
2. Remove bowl from heat and mix in honey.
3. Allow mixture to cool and thicken a bit, then pour over the frosting layer. Place brownies in freezer to set the toppings.

Tip: You can bake the brownie layer 1-2 days (or even up to a week) in advance . To store them, simply freeze the brownies wrapped in parchment paper, then in foil, and finally in a ziploc bag. Pull out to thaw the day before you prepare the toppings.

CLASSIC WALNUT BROWNIES

🍴 SERVES: 12-16 🕐 PREP: 20 MINS 🕐 COOK: 30 MINS

INGREDIENTS:

- ¾ cup walnut halves and pieces, divided
- ⅓ cup coconut oil, melted
- 4 oz unsweetened baking chocolate
- 1 cup almond flour
- 1 cup coconut sugar
- 3 eggs
- 1 tbsp vanilla extract

METHOD:

1. Preheat oven to 350°F.
2. Chop and toast ½ cup walnuts on 350°F until browned, about 10 minutes. Remove from heat and set aside.
3. Line an 8x8x2-inch baking dish with parchment paper and set aside.
4. In a small saucepan, heat the coconut oil and chocolate over low heat until melted. When the chocolate and oil are melted, remove from heat and set aside.
5. In a medium bowl, combine the almond flour and coconut sugar and mix to incorporate.
6. Add the melted chocolate and oil and mix.
7. Add the eggs and vanilla and mix to completely combine. Fold in the toasted walnuts
8. Pour the batter into the prepared pan and spread it to fit the pan.
9. Use the remaining walnut pieces and halves to top the batter.
10. Bake at 350°F for 25-30 minutes, until a toothpick inserted in the middle comes out clean.
11. Remove brownies from the oven and cool completely on a wire rack before slicing.

MEXICAN HOT CHOCOLATE BROWNIES

SERVES: 12-16 **PREP: 15 MINS** **COOK: 30 MINS**

INGREDIENTS:

- ½ cup cacao nibs, divided
- ⅓ cup coconut oil, melted
- 4 oz unsweetened baking chocolate
- 1 cup almond flour
- 2 tsp cinnamon, plus extra for dusting
- ¼ tsp cayenne pepper
- ½ tsp ancho chili powder
- ¼ tsp nutmeg
- ¼ tsp ground coffee or espresso
- 1 cup coconut sugar
- 3 eggs
- 1 tbsp vanilla extract

METHOD:

1. Preheat oven to 350°F.

2. Spread the cacao nibs in a single layer on a baking sheet. Bake for 7-10 minutes, until the oils are released (you can tell when this happens because the nibs get shiny). Remove the toasted cacao nibs from the oven and set aside to cool.

3. Line an 8x8x2-inch baking dish with parchment paper and set aside.

4. In a small saucepan, heat the coconut oil and chocolate over low heat until melted. When the chocolate and oil are melted, remove from heat and set aside.

5. In a medium bowl combine the almond flour, spices, coffee, and coconut sugar and mix to incorporate.

6. Add melted chocolate and oil and mix.

7. Add eggs and vanilla and mix to completely combine. Fold in ⅓ cup of the toasted cacao nibs.

8. Scoop the batter into the prepared baking dish and spread to fit the dish. Sprinkle the remaining cacao nibs over the batter in an even layer.

9. Bake the brownies for 25-30 minutes, until a toothpick inserted into the middle comes out mostly clean.

S'MORES BROWNIES

 SERVES: 12-16 PREP: 1 HR 30 MINS COOK: 1 HR

INGREDIENTS:

Graham Crust Layer

- ¾ cup almond flour
- ½ cup arrowroot starch
- 1 tbsp coconut flour
- ¼ tsp salt
- ½ tsp baking soda
- 3 tbsp honey
- ¼ cup melted coconut oil
- 1 tbsp molasses

Brownie Layer

- 2½ tbsp coconut oil
- 2 oz unsweetened baking chocolate
- ½ cup almond flour
- ½ cup coconut sugar
- 2 eggs
- ½ tbsp vanilla extract

Marshmallow Layer

- ½ cup water, divided
- 1½ tbsp gelatin
- ½ cup white wildflower honey
- ½ tsp vanilla
- ¼ tsp salt

METHOD:

Prepare the crust:

1. Preheat the oven to 350°F. Line an 8x8x2-inch baking dish with parchment paper and set aside.

2. Combine almond flour, arrowroot, coconut flour, salt, and baking soda in a medium bowl. Mix well to combine.

3. In a small bowl combine honey, coconut oil, and molasses and stir to completely mix. Add honey mixture to dry ingredients and mix to form a dough.

4. Press the dough into the prepared baking dish and bake for 25 minutes.

Prepare the brownie batter:

1. While the crust is baking, place coconut oil and chocolate in a small saucepan and heat over low until melted.

2. In a medium bowl combine almond flour and coconut sugar and mix to combine. Stir in melted chocolate mixture.

3. Add eggs and vanilla and mix until completely combined and smooth.

4. When the crust is finished baking, pour the brownie batter over the graham cracker crust and bake at 350°F for 15-20 minutes.

5. Allow the brownies to cool completely before adding the marshmallow layer.

Prepare the marshmallow layer:

1. Pour ½ of the water into a large, clean bowl or the bowl of a stand mixer. Sprinkle gelatin over water and allow it to hydrate.

2. While the gelatin is hydrating, combine honey, vanilla, salt, and remaining water in a small saucepan and heat over medium-low about 10 minutes. Stir occasionally to keep the mixture from bubbling over.

3. When the honey mixture is ready, remove it from heat. Using an electric or stand mixer, whip the gelatin mixture on medium as you very slowly pour in the warm honey mixture (make sure to do this slowly to give the gelatin time to dissolve).

4. When the honey mixture is completely added, turn the mixer up to high and continue to beat until the mixture doubles or triples in volume and begins to develop a marshmallow fluff consistency, about 5-10 minutes.

5. When the mixture is ready, spread it over the cooled brownie layer. Place the brownies in the fridge and allow to chill and set 1 hour (or overnight).

To serve:

1. Turn the oven broiler on high, or use a crème brûlée torch.

2. Broil on high close to the burner, turning occasionally, about 5 minutes, until the top begins to brown. Keep a close eye on the marshmallow as it may burn.

3. If using a crème brûlée torch, hold the torch approximately 3 inches from the surface of the marshmallow and move evenly over the entire top to brown.

4. Allow the brownies to set again in the fridge 15 minutes before slicing and serving.

"PEANUT BUTTER" SWIRL BROWNIES

SERVES: 12-16   **PREP: 10 MINS**   **COOK: 30 MINS**

INGREDIENTS:

Brownies

- ⅓ cup coconut oil, melted
- 4 oz unsweetened baking chocolate
- 1 cup almond flour
- 1 cup coconut sugar
- ¼ tsp salt
- 3 eggs
- 1 tbsp vanilla extract

Filling

- ¾ cup almond butter
- 2½ tsp toasted sesame oil
- 2 tbsp nutritional yeast
- ½ tsp salt
- 1 tsp vanilla
- 2 tbsp honey

METHOD:

1. Preheat the oven to 350°F. Line an 8x8x2-inch baking dish with parchment paper and set aside.

2. In a small saucepan, heat coconut oil and chocolate over low heat until melted. Remove the pan from heat and set aside.

3. In a medium bowl, combine almond flour, coconut sugar, and salt. Stir.

4. Add melted chocolate mixture and stir.

5. Add eggs and vanilla and mix to completely combine.

6. Pour ½ of the brownie batter in the prepared baking dish and spread to an even layer. Using a spoon, dollop ⅓ of the almond butter filling onto the batter and swirl. Top with remaining brownie batter, then dollop leftover almond butter filling in a different pattern and swirl.

7. Bake for 30 minutes, then remove from the oven and cool completely before slicing and serving.

FLOURLESS FUDGE BROWNIE BITES

SERVES: 16-25   PREP: 5 MINS   COOK: 1 HR 10 MINS

INGREDIENTS:

- 1 cup almond butter
- ¾ cup + 2 Tbsp maple syrup
- 1 tsp baking powder
- ¼ tsp sea salt
- ¾ cup cacao powder
- 1 tbsp vanilla

METHOD:

1. Preheat the oven to 325°F. Line an 8x8x2" baking dish with parchment paper and set aside.

2. Combine all ingredients in a medium bowl and mix to completely combine.

3. Spread the batter into the prepared baking dish.

4. Bake 60-70 minutes, until the top of the brownies is set and shiny, and toothpick inserted in the center of the brownies comes out mostly clean.

5. Allow the brownies to cool in the pan until firm enough to transfer, then transfer them to a wire rack to cool completely.

6. Carefully remove the parchment paper once the brownies are completely cooled, and slice into squares using a sharp knife.

7. Enjoy!

cake

WALNUT CAKE WITH COFFEE FROSTING

🍴 **SERVES: 12-16** 🕐 **PREP: 15 MINS** 🕐 **COOK: 30 MINS**

INGREDIENTS:

- ¼ cup arrowroot starch, plus extra for flouring the cake pan
- 5 eggs
- ¼ cup coconut oil
- ½ cup honey
- 3 tbsp almond milk
- 1 tbsp vanilla
- 1 tbsp apple cider vinegar
- ½ cup coconut flour
- ½ tsp baking soda
- 1 tsp baking powder
- ¼ tsp salt
- ⅓ cup chopped walnuts, toasted
- ½ cup walnut butter

Coffee Frosting

- 2 tbsp maple syrup
- ½ tsp vanilla
- 4 tbsp arrowroot starch
- 1 tbsp collagen
- ½ cup coconut cream
- 1 tsp decaf coffee crystals

METHOD:

Prepare the cake:

1. Preheat the oven to 350°F. Oil an 8-inch round cake pan, dust it with arrowroot, and line the bottom with parchment paper. Set aside.
2. In a large bowl, combine eggs, oil, honey, almond milk, vanilla, walnut butter and apple cider vinegar. Whisk the mixture until smooth and completely combined.
3. In a small bowl combine coconut flour, arrowroot, baking soda, baking powder, and salt. Mix to completely combine.
4. Add dry ingredients to wet ingredients and mix to incorporate. The mixture will be lumpy—let it sit for 2-3 minutes, then mix again until smooth.
5. Fold in walnuts.
6. Pour the batter into the oiled and lined cake pan.
7. Bake 25-30 minutes, until a toothpick inserted in the center of the cake comes out clean.
8. Remove from the oven and allow to cool in the pan 5-10 minutes. Turn the cake out of the pan to cool completely on a wire rack.

To prepare the frosting:

1. Combine the arrowroot, maple syrup, collagen, and vanilla in a small saucepan and heat over low. Stir constantly until the mixture begins to thicken, 3-5 minutes. Set aside to cool.
2. In a small bowl, whisk coconut cream with coffee. Add to maple syrup mixture and whip with an electric mixer or a whisk until completely combined.
3. Spread frosting over the top of the cooled walnut cake, and decorate with extra walnut pieces if desired.

SEXY BLACK FOREST CAKE

🍴 SERVES: 12-16 🕐 PREP: 40 MINS 🕐 COOK: 30 MINS

INGREDIENTS:

Chocolate Cake

- Arrowroot starch, for dusting
- 10 eggs
- ⅔ cup coconut oil
- 1 cup maple syrup
- ⅓ cup almond milk
- 2 tbsp vanilla
- 2 tbsp apple cider vinegar
- 1 cup coconut flour
- ½ cup cacao powder
- 1 tsp baking soda
- 2 tsp baking powder
- ½ tsp salt

Cherry Whipped Cream

- 4 tbsp kirschwasser
- 1 tbsp gelatin
- 8 oz frozen dark cherries, thawed
- ¼ cup boiling water
- 2 cups coconut cream
- ¼ cup honey
- 1 tsp lemon juice
- ¼ tsp decaf espresso

Chocolate Ganache

- 4 oz unsweetened baking chocolate
- ⅓ cup coconut oil
- ¼ cup honey

METHOD:

To prepare the cake:

1. Preheat the oven to 350°F. Oil two 8-inch round cake pans, dust them with arrowroot, and line the bottom with parchment paper. Set aside.

2. In a large bowl, combine eggs, oil, maple syrup, almond milk, vanilla, and apple cider vinegar. Whisk the mixture until it's smooth and completely combined.

3. In a small bowl combine coconut flour, cacao powder, baking soda, baking powder, and salt. Mix to completely combine.

4. Add dry ingredients to wet ingredients and mix to incorporate. The mixture will be lumpy—let it sit for 2-3 minutes, then mix again until smooth.

5. Pour the batter into the oiled and lined cake pans.

6. Bake 25-30 minutes, until a toothpick inserted in the center of the cake comes out clean.

7. Remove from the oven and allow to cool in the pans 5-10 minutes. Turn the cakes out of the pans to cool completely on a wire rack.

To prepare the whipped filling:

1. Pour the kirschwasser into a small bowl. Sprinkle the gelatin over the kirschwasser to allow it to "hydrate."

2. While the gelatin is hydrating, chop the cherries and set them aside.

3. Add boiling water to the kirschwasser and gelatin and stir to dissolve.

4. Combine all ingredients except the chopped cherries in a medium bowl, and whip until the mixture is light and fluffy.

5. Fold the chopped cherries into the whipped cream. Transfer the bowl to the fridge and chill until set, 1 hour (or overnight).

To prepare the ganache:

1. Combine all ingredients in the bowl of a double boiler.

2. Heat over medium until ingredients are melted.

3. Stir to combine, then remove the bowl from the heat and allow the ganache to cool while you assemble the cake.

To assemble:

1. While the cake is baking, prepare the whipped cherry filling and allow to set and chill in the fridge.

2. Carefully use a serrated knife to cut the cake layers in half through the middle (creating 4 cake layers).

3. Plate the first layer of cake and spoon ½ - ⅔ cup of the whipped topping onto the layer. Spread the whipped topping evenly over the layer, then repeat with the remaining cake layers and whipped topping, finishing with the top cake layer.

4. Place the cake in the fridge to set.

5. Once the ganache has cooled, remove cake from the fridge and pour the ganache over the top, carefully tilting the cake to drizzle the ganache down the sides.

6. Chill to set, about 30 minutes. Remove the cake from the fridge 15 minutes before serving to allow the ganache to soften.

CARROT CAKE

🍴 SERVES: 12-16　🕐 PREP: 1 HR 20 MINS　🕐 COOK: 45 MINS

INGREDIENTS:

- ¼ cup arrowroot starch, plus extra for flouring the cake pans
- 8 eggs
- ½ cup coconut oil
- ⅔ cup honey
- ¼ cup applesauce
- 1 tsp orange zest
- 1 tbsp fresh grated ginger
- 1 tbsp vanilla
- 1 tbsp apple cider vinegar
- ¾ cup coconut flour
- 2 tsp cinnamon
- ¼ tsp nutmeg
- ¼ tsp cardamom
- 1 tsp baking soda
- 2 tsp baking powder
- ½ tsp salt
- 2 cups shredded carrots
- ½ cup walnuts
- ½ cup raisins

METHOD:

1. Preheat the oven to 350°F. Oil two 8-inch round cake pans, dust them with arrowroot starch, and line the bottom with parchment paper. Set aside.

2. In a large bowl combine eggs, oil, honey, applesauce, orange zest, ginger, vanilla, and apple cider vinegar. Whisk the mixture until it's smooth and completely combined.

3. In a small bowl combine the coconut flour, arrowroot, spices, baking soda, baking powder, and salt. Mix to completely combine.

4. Add the dry ingredients to the wet ingredients and mix to incorporate. The mixture will be lumpy—let it sit for 2-3 minutes, then mix again until smooth.

5. Fold in carrots, walnuts, and raisins.

6. Pour the batter into the oiled and lined cake pans.

7. Bake 40-45 minutes, until a toothpick inserted in the center of the cake comes out clean.

8. Remove from the oven and allow to cool in the pans 5-10 minutes. Turn the cakes out of the pans to cool completely on a wire rack.

Cashew Cream Cheese Frosting

- ½ cup water + ¼ cup boiling water
- 1½ tbsp gelatin
- 3 cups cashews, soaked overnight
- ¾ cup coconut cream
- 1 tbsp apple cider vinegar
- 4 tbsp lemon juice
- 1 tsp lemon zest
- 1 tsp vanilla
- ¼ tsp salt
- ½ cup honey

Prepare the cashew cream cheese frosting:

1. Add the ½ cup water to a small bowl. Sprinkle the gelatin over the water to allow it to hydrate, and set it aside.

2. While the gelatin is hydrating, combine remaining ingredients in a high-powered blender.

3. When the gelatin is hydrated, add the ¼ cup boiling water to the bowl and stir to dissolve gelatin. Add gelatin to the blender and blend everything until it is smooth and creamy.

4. Pour the frosting into a bowl and place it in the fridge 4 hours (or overnight) to set.

5. Whip the frosting with an electric mixer before icing the cake. Once the cake is iced, place in the fridge to set, about 1 hour, before serving.

BANANA BUNDT CAKE

SERVES: 12-16   **PREP: 10 MINS**   **COOK: 1 HR**

INGREDIENTS:

Sesame Caramel Glaze

- ¼ cup ghee
- ¼ cup + 1 tbsp coconut sugar
- 2 tbsp full-fat coconut milk
- 1 tsp vanilla
- Pinch of sea salt
- 2 tbsp tahini
- 1 tsp toasted sesame oil
- 1 tsp white sesame seeds, to garnish

Cake

- ¼ cup coconut oil, melted, plus extra for oiling the pan
- 3 tbsp arrowroot starch, plus extra for dusting the pan
- 8 eggs
- ¼ cup honey
- 4 grams powdered stevia
- 1 cup mashed banana
- 1 tbsp vanilla
- 1 tbsp lemon juice
- ¾ cup + 3 tbsp coconut flour
- 1 tsp baking soda
- 2 tsp baking powder
- ½ tsp salt
- 6 oz freeze-dried bananas, crushed

METHOD:

Prepare the glaze first:

1. Combine all ingredients in a small saucepan over medium-low heat until ghee is melted, stirring occasionally to combine.

2. When the mixture is smooth and completely mixed, remove it from heat and allow to cool while you prepare the cake.

To prepare the cake:

1. Preheat the oven to 350°F. Oil a 6-cup Bundt pan, dust it with arrowroot starch, and set aside.

2. In a large bowl, combine eggs, oil, honey, stevia, mashed banana, vanilla, and lemon juice. Whisk until smooth and completely combined.

3. In a small bowl combine coconut flour, arrowroot, baking soda, baking powder, and salt. Mix to completely combine.

4. Add dry ingredients to wet ingredients and mix to incorporate. The mixture will be lumpy—let it sit for 2-3 minutes, then mix again until smooth.

5. Fold in the crushed freeze-dried bananas.

6. Pour the batter into the oiled Bundt pan.

7. Bake 50-60 minutes, until a toothpick inserted in the center of the cake comes out clean.

8. Remove from the oven and allow to cool in the pan for 5-10 minutes. Turn the cake out of the pan to cool slightly on a wire rack.

9. Plate the cake and pour caramel glaze over the cake while warm (for best absorption). Serve warm or at room temperature.

VANILLA CAKE WITH MATCHA GREEN TEA FROSTING

SERVES: 12-16   PREP: 15 MINS   COOK: 30 MINS

INGREDIENTS:

Matcha Green Tea Frosting

- 1 cup arrowroot starch
- ⅔ cup honey
- ⅓ cup maple syrup
- 2 tbsp + 2 tsp matcha green tea powder
- 2 cups palm shortening

Cake

- ½ cup arrowroot starch, plus extra for flouring the cake pans
- 10 eggs
- ⅔ cup coconut oil
- ½ cup honey
- ⅓ cup almond milk
- 2 tbsp vanilla
- Zest of ½ a lemon (about ¼ - ½ tsp)
- 2 tbsp lemon juice
- 1 cup coconut flour
- 1 tsp baking soda
- 2 tsp baking powder
- ½ tsp salt

METHOD:

To prepare the frosting:

1. Combine arrowroot, honey, maple syrup, and matcha in a medium bowl and whisk until no lumps remain.
2. Using an electric mixer or a whisk, whip in palm shortening until smooth.
3. Set the frosting aside while you prepare the cake.

To prepare the cake:

1. Preheat the oven to 350°F. Oil two 8-inch round cake pans, dust them with arrowroot, and line the bottom with parchment paper. Set aside.
2. In a large bowl, combine eggs, oil, honey, almond milk, vanilla, lemon zest, and lemon juice. Whisk the mixture until it's smooth and completely combined.
3. In a small bowl combine coconut flour, arrowroot, baking soda, baking powder, and salt. Mix to completely combine.
4. Add dry ingredients to wet ingredients and mix to incorporate. The mixture will be lumpy—let it sit for 2-3 minutes, then mix again until smooth.
5. Pour the batter into the oiled and lined cake pans.
6. Bake 25-30 minutes, until a toothpick inserted in the center of the cake comes out clean.
7. Remove from the oven and allow to cool in the pans 5-10 minutes. Turn the cakes out of the pans to cool completely on a wire rack before frosting.

CHOCOLATE CHIP COOKIE CAKE

🍴 SERVES: 12-16 🕐 PREP: 45 MINS 🕐 COOK: 40 MINS

INGREDIENTS:

Chocolate Chips

- 2 oz unsweetend baking chocolate
- 1 oz cacao butter
- 2 tbsp honey

Cake

- 2 eggs
- ¼ cup palm shortening, melted
- 2 tsp vanilla
- 2 cups almond flour
- ¼ cup arrowroot
- ½ cup coconut sugar
- ½ tsp baking soda
- ¼ tsp salt

Piping Frosting

- 1 tbsp arrowroot starch
- 2 tbsp honey or maple syrup
- ¼ cup palm shortening
- ½ oz unsweetened baking chocolate

METHOD:

Prepare the chocolate chips.

1. Line a baking sheet or dinner plate with parchment paper and set aside.

2. Combine all ingredients in the bowl of a double boiler and heat over medium until melted.

3. When ingredients are melted, remove the bowl from the pot and stir to mix completely.

4. Pour melted chocolate mixture onto the prepared baking sheet or plate and place in the fridge to set, 30 minutes or overnight. Use a sharp knife to chop the chocolate into small chunks. Store in the fridge.

Tip: The chocolate chunks may be made up to 3-4 days in advance.

To prepare the cake:

1. Preheat the oven to 350°F. Oil 1x 8-inch round cake pan and line the bottom with parchment paper. Set aside.

2. In a small bowl, combine eggs, shortening, and vanilla. Whisk until smooth.

3. In a medium bowl combine almond flour, arrowroot, coconut sugar, baking soda, and salt. Mix to completely combine.

4. Add wet ingredients to dry ingredients and mix to incorporate. Stir until smooth.

5. Fold in the chocolate chunks.

6. Pour the dough into the oiled and lined cake pan and press the dough to fit the pan.

7. Bake 35-40 minutes, until a toothpick inserted in the center of the cake comes out clean.

8. Remove from the oven and allow to cool in the pan 5-10 minutes. Turn the cake out of the pan, flip upright, and leave to cool completely on a wire rack.

To prepare the piping frosting:

1. In a small bowl whisk arrowroot and maple syrup. Set aside.

2. Combine shortening and chocolate in a small saucepan and heat over low until melted. Remove from heat and stir to combine.

3. Add melted chocolate and shortening to the maple syrup mixture and stir to combine.

4. Leave the frosting to set before piping.

To frost the cake:

1. Cut the corner off of a 1-quart ziploc bag. Either fit the end with a cake frosting tip or leave as is.

2. Spoon the frosting into the prepared ziploc bag. Squeeze the frosting toward the prepared tip of the bag, squeezing out any air.

3. Frost the cake as desired.

APPLE SKILLET CAKE

 SERVES: 12-16   PREP: 25 MINS   COOK: 25 MINS

INGREDIENTS:

- 2 tbsp coconut oil or ghee, melted
- 4 baking apples, peeled, seeded, and quartered, reserving ½ of one apple
- 5 eggs
- ½ cup coconut oil
- ⅓ cup maple syrup
- 1 tsp vanilla
- 1 tbsp + 2 tsp lemon juice
- ½ cup coconut flour
- ¼ cup arrowroot starch
- ⅛ tsp nutmeg
- ⅛ tsp clove
- ½ tsp baking soda
- 1 tsp baking powder
- ¼ tsp salt

METHOD:

Prepare the apples:

1. Combine the 2 tablespoons coconut oil or ghee in a cast iron or other oven-proof skillet and heat over medium-high heat.
2. Place apple quarters in a circle on their flat side, spiraling around the center piece. Place the reserved ½ apple cut side up in the middle. Sear on high about 3 minutes to brown the apples, then reduce heat to medium and continue to cook 10 minutes, until apples start to soften.

To make the batter:

1. Preheat the oven to 350°F.
2. In a large bowl, combine eggs, oil, maple syrup, vanilla, and lemon juice. Whisk the mixture until it's smooth and completely combined.
3. In a small bowl combine coconut flour, arrowroot, spices, baking soda, baking powder, and salt. Mix to completely combine.
4. Add dry ingredients to wet ingredients and mix to incorporate. The mixture will be lumpy—let it sit for 2-3 minutes, then mix again until smooth.
5. Pour batter over cooked apples in the skillet. Transfer the skillet to the oven.
6. Bake 20-25 minutes, until cake is golden and set on top. Remove cake from the oven.
7. Place a large plate or serving platter, serving side down, over the skillet.
8. Carefully flip the skillet to turn out the cake onto the plate. Serve warm.

Note: Alternatively, you could prepare the apples in a non-oven proof skillet, then arrange the cooked apples in a 9-inch cake pan and follow the rest of the directions through, baking the cake in the cake pan.

PINEAPPLE UPSIDE-DOWN CAKE

SERVES: 12-16   PREP: 10 MINS   COOK: 30 MINS

INGREDIENTS:

Caramel

- 3 tbsp butter or ghee
- 3 tbsp coconut palm sugar
- 1 tbsp water

Cake

- 7 sliced pineapple rings
- 7 cherries
- 5 eggs
- ½ cup coconut oil
- ⅓ cup honey
- 1 tbsp vanilla
- 1 tbsp lemon juice
- ½ cup coconut flour
- ¼ cup arrowroot starch
- ½ tsp baking soda
- 1 tsp baking powder
- ¼ tsp salt

METHOD:

Preheat the oven to 350°F.

To prepare the caramel:

1. Begin by combining all ingredients in a small saucepan and heating over medium heat. Stir to completely combine all ingredients as the ghee melts.
2. When the caramel is smooth, heat to simmer 2-3 minutes to thicken.
3. Pour the prepared caramel into a 9-inch cake pan and spread to coat the bottom of the pan evenly.
4. Arrange pineapple rings around the bottom of the cake pan, with one ring in the center. Place a cherry in the center of each of the pineapple rings. Set aside.

To prepare the cake:

1. In a large bowl, combine eggs, oil, honey, vanilla, and lemon juice. Whisk the mixture until it's smooth and completely combined.
2. In a small bowl combine coconut flour, arrowroot, baking soda, baking powder, and salt. Mix to completely combine.
3. Add dry ingredients to wet ingredients and mix to incorporate. The mixture will be lumpy—let it sit for 2-3 minutes, then mix again until smooth.
4. Pour the batter over the pineapple rings in the cake pan.
5. Bake 25-30 minutes, until cake is golden and set on top.
6. Remove pan from the oven. Run a knife along the inside of the pan to loosen it.
7. Place a plate, serving side down onto the cake pan. Carefully flip the hot cake pan onto the plate so the cake is released.
8. Allow the cake to cool slightly before serving. Serve warm or at room temperature.

PECAN CRUMBLE COFFEE CAKE

🍴 SERVES: 12-16 🕐 PREP: 10 MINS 🕐 COOK: 45 MINS

INGREDIENTS:

- 6 eggs
- ¼ cup coconut oil
- ⅓ cup applesauce
- ⅓ cup maple syrup
- 2 tsp vanilla
- ¾ cup coconut flour
- 1 tsp baking soda
- 1 tbsp cinnamon
- Dash of sea salt

Crumble Topping

- 1 cup pecans, chopped
- ½ cup almond flour
- 1-2 tsp cinnamon, optional
- Dash of sea salt
- ¼ cup maple syrup
- ¼ cup coconut oil

METHOD:

1. Preheat the oven to 350°F. Line an 8x8x2-inch baking dish with parchment paper. Set aside.

2. In a large bowl, combine eggs, oil, applesauce, maple syrup, and vanilla. Whisk the mixture until it's smooth and completely combined.

3. In a small bowl, combine coconut flour, baking soda, cinnamon, and salt. Mix to completely combine.

4. Add dry ingredients to wet ingredients and mix to incorporate. The mixture will be lumpy—let it sit for 2-3 minutes, then mix again until smooth.

5. Pour the batter into the lined baking dish.

6. In a small bowl, combine crumble topping ingredients and mix completely.

7. Spread crumble mixture evenly over the cake batter.

8. Bake 40-45 minutes, until a toothpick inserted in the center of the cake comes out clean.

9. Remove from the oven and allow to cool in the pan 5-10 minutes before removing to cool on a wire rack.

LEMON CAKE WITH MARSHMALLOW-MERINGUE FROSTING

🍴 SERVES: 12-16 🕐 PREP: 1 HR 🕐 COOK: 45 MINS

INGREDIENTS:

Lemon Curd
- ½ cup honey
- ⅓ cup fresh lemon juice
- 1 large egg
- 1 large egg yolk
- 1 tbsp collagen
- 3 tbsp coconut oil

Lemon Cake
- ½ cup arrowroot starch, plus extra for dusting
- 10 eggs
- 2/3 cup coconut oil
- ¾ cup honey
- ⅓ cup almond milk
- ¼ cup applesauce
- 1 tbsp vanilla
- 1 tbsp fresh lemon zest
- 3 tbsp lemon juice
- 1 cup coconut flour
- 1 tsp baking soda
- 2 tsp baking powder
- ½ tsp salt

Marshmallow-Meringue Frosting
- 1½ tsp gelatin
- 2 tbsp water
- 2 egg whites
- ½ cup white wildflower honey
- ½ tsp vanilla
- ¼ tsp salt

METHOD:

Prepare the lemon curd:

1. In a small saucepan whisk together honey and lemon juice. Heat over medium until just simmering.

2. In a medium bowl, whisk eggs, collagen, and oil until they are smooth.

3. Slowly pour the honey mixture into the egg mixture, whisking constantly, to temper the eggs.

4. Return mixture to the saucepan and heat on medium-low heat. Cook until thick, about 15 minutes, whisking constantly.

5. When the lemon curd is thickened, transfer it to a container and press plastic wrap onto the top to prevent a film from forming. Allow to cool, then put the container in the fridge to set completely.

Tip: You can make the lemon curd 1-2 days ahead.

To make the cake:

1. Preheat the oven to 350°F. Oil two 8-inch round cake pans, dust them with arrowroot, and line the bottom with parchment paper. Set aside.

2. In a large bowl, combine eggs, oil, honey, almond milk, applesauce, vanilla, lemon zest, and lemon juice. Whisk the mixture until it's smooth and completely combined.

3. In a small bowl combine coconut flour, arrowroot, baking soda, baking powder, and salt. Mix to completely combine.

4. Add dry ingredients to wet ingredients and mix to incorporate. The mixture will be lumpy—let it sit for about 3 minutes, then mix again until smooth.

5. Pour batter into the oiled and lined cake pans.

6. Bake 40-45 minutes, until a toothpick inserted in the center of the cake comes out clean.

7. Remove from the oven and allow to cool in the pan 5-10 minutes. Turn the cakes out of the pans to cool completely on a wire rack.

To assemble the cake:

1. Plate the first layer of the cake. Spread lemon curd evenly over the bottom cake layer, leaving about ¼-inch of space around the edge (the lemon curd will spread as you place the top layer on).

2. Place the top layer onto the lemon curd. Follow frosting directions.

To make the frosting:

(Note: assemble the cake before you prepare the marshmallow frosting—the frosting sets very quickly!)

1. In a small bowl, sprinkle gelatin over water to dissolve. Set aside.

2. Place egg whites in a large clean bowl and use an electric mixer to beat them until they are stiff. Set aside.

3. Heat honey, vanilla, and salt in a small saucepan over medium heat until it just boils, then remove it from the heat.

4. Add gelatin mixture to egg whites and begin to beat on low speed while slowly pouring in the hot honey. Continue to beat until the mixture forms stiff peaks and is fluffy.

5. Allow the frosting to set 5-10 minutes, then frost the cake. Transfer the cake to the fridge for about 30 minutes to allow the frosting to set completely before slicing and serving.

SOUTHERN CHOCOLATE POUND CAKE

🍴 SERVES: 12-16 🕐 PREP: 15 MINS 🕐 COOK: 1 HR

INGREDIENTS:

- ½ cup coconut oil, plus extra for greasing
- Arrowroot, for dusting
- 6 eggs
- 1 tsp vanilla extract
- ¾ cup applesauce
- ½ cup full-fat coconut milk
- 1 cup coconut flour, sifted
- ⅓ cup cacao powder
- ¼ cup coconut sugar
- 4 grams powdered stevia
- 2 tsp baking powder
- 1 tsp baking soda

METHOD:

1. Preheat the oven to 350°F. Grease a Bundt pan with coconut oil and dust it with arrowroot. Set aside.

2. In a medium-large bowl combine eggs, vanilla extract, applesauce, coconut milk, and coconut oil. Stir to completely combine.

3. In a smaller bowl, mix coconut flour, cacao powder, coconut sugar, stevia, baking powder, and baking soda.

4. Slowly add dry ingredients to wet ingredients and stir well to combine. The batter will be lumpy at first—let it sit for 5-10 minutes after the initial mixing and then repeat until the batter is smooth.

5. Pour batter into the prepared pan. Bake 45-60 minutes, testing to see if a toothpick comes out clean. Store in an airtight container in the fridge for up to 5 days.

MINI FLOURLESS CHOCOLATE CAKES

SERVES: 12-16 **PREP: 5 MINS** **COOK: 20 MINS**

INGREDIENTS:

- 4 oz unsweetened baking chocolate
- ½ cup coconut oil or ghee
- 6 egg whites (about 1 cup egg whites)
- ¼ tsp salt
- ½ cup honey
- 2-4 grams powdered stevia
- 1 tsp vanilla extract
- ¼ cup cacao powder

METHOD:

1. Preheat the oven to 375°F. Line a muffin tin with parchment paper, use silicone muffin liners, or oil very, very, very well. Set aside.

2. In a small saucepan, melt chocolate and oil over medium heat.

3. While chocolate is melting, whip egg whites with salt in a medium bowl until they become frothy. Add honey, stevia, vanilla extract, and cacao powder and continue to whip until just combined.

4. When chocolate and oil are melted, gently fold the mixture into the egg white mixture until just combined.

5. Evenly divide batter between muffin cups. Bake 15-20 minutes, until the center of the mini cakes are just set.

6. Serve warm or cooled with a dollop of coconut whipped cream or a simple dusting of "powdered sugar" (1 tbsp arrowroot starch + 1 packet powdered stevia) and some fresh berries.

7. Store in an airtight container in the fridge up to 5 days.

cheesecakes

CHOCOLATE NO-BAKE CHEESECAKE

🍴 SERVES: 12-16   🕐 PREP: 5 HRS   🕐 COOK: 0 MINS

INGREDIENTS:

Crust

- 1 cup pecans or hazelnuts
- ½ cup shredded coconut
- 2 tbsp cacao powder
- ¼ tsp salt
- 1 cup dates, chopped
- 2 tbsp coconut oil, melted

Filling

- 2 cup cashews, soaked overnight
- 7 oz unsweetened baking chocolate OR cacao paste, melted
- ½ cup + 2 tbsp maple syrup
- 1 cup coconut cream
- 3 tbsp lemon juice
- 1 tbsp vanilla

METHOD:

Prepare the crust:

1. Line an 8-inch springform pan with parchment paper and set aside.
2. Process nuts into a flour in food processor fitted with an "S" blade. Add coconut, cacao, and salt and process again. Set aside.
3. Process dates into a paste, then add ground nut mixture and oil to date paste and process to form a crumbly but sticky dough.
4. Press dough into an even layer on the bottom of the prepared 8-inch springform pan.
5. Place crust in the fridge to set, 30 minutes (or overnight).

Prepare the filling:

1. Combine all ingredients in a high powered blender and blend until smooth.
2. Pour filling over prepared crust. Transfer the cake to the fridge to set, 4 hours (or overnight).

GRAHAM CRACKER CRUST

🍴 SERVES: 12-16 🕐 PREP: 5 MINS 🕐 COOK: 15 MINS

INGREDIENTS:

- 1 batch graham crackers (page 91)
- 1 egg white

METHOD:

1. Preheat the oven to 350°F.

2. Break graham crackers into pieces and place in the bowl of a food processor fitted with an "S" blade.

3. Process graham crackers into a powder.

4. While the food processor is on, add egg white to graham cracker powder and process just until combined.

5. Pour mixture into an 8-inch springform pan and press into an even layer.

6. Bake 15 minutes, until the crust is set. Allow to cool completely before adding cheesecake filling.

CLASSIC VANILLA CHEESECAKE

🍴 **SERVES: 12-16** 🕐 **PREP: 7 HRS** 🕐 **COOK: 2 HRS**

INGREDIENTS:

- 1 graham cracker crust (page 49)

Filling

- 1 cup cashews, soaked overnight
- ½ lb zucchini, peeled and chopped
- ½ cup honey
- ⅓ cup coconut oil
- ⅔ cup coconut cream
- ¼ cup lemon juice
- 1½ tsp apple cider vinegar
- 3 eggs
- 2 tsp vanilla
- ¼ tsp vanilla powder
- 3 tbsp arrowroot starch

METHOD:

1. Preheat the oven to 350°F.

2. Combine all ingredients in a high-powered blender or food processor and blend until smooth and creamy.

3. Pour filling over prepared crust.

4. Put the springform pan on a square of aluminum foil that's set in a baking dish. Fold the foil up to cover the sides of the springform pan, and fill the baking dish with 3 cups boiling water.

5. Place the whole baking dish in the oven on the middle rack. Bake 20 minutes in the water bath, then reduce the heat to 250°F and bake an additional 90 minutes, until the center is completely set.

6. Turn off oven and crack the door to allow the cake to cool slowly. Leave for about 1 hour (cooling the cake slowly prevents cracks on top of the cake). When the cake is cool enough to handle, transfer it to the fridge and chill 6 hours (or overnight) to fully set.

DULCE DE LECHE CHEESECAKE

🍴 SERVES: 12-16 🕐 PREP: 7 HRS 🕐 COOK: 2 HRS

INGREDIENTS:

- 1 graham cracker crust (page 49)

Caramel Sauce

- ½ cup butter
- ¾ cup coconut sugar
- 2 tbsp water
- 2 tbsp coconut cream
- 1 tsp vanilla

Filling

- 1 cup cashews, soaked overnight
- ½ lb zucchini, peeled and chopped
- Remaining caramel sauce (about ¾ c)
- ½ cup coconut oil
- ½ cup coconut cream
- ¼ cup lemon juice
- 3 eggs
- 1 tsp vanilla
- 3 tbsp arrowroot starch

METHOD:

1. Preheat the oven to 350°F.
2. Combine all caramel sauce ingredients in a small saucepan and heat until the butter is melted, stirring occasionally. After mixture is smooth and combined, continue stirring to allow caramel to thicken, 3-5 minutes.
3. Remove caramel from heat and set aside to cool while you prepare the filling.
4. Combine all ingredients except ½ cup of the caramel sauce in a high-powered blender or food processor and blend until smooth and creamy.
5. Pour filling over prepared crust.
6. Put the springform pan on a square of aluminum foil set in a baking dish. Fold foil up to cover sides of springform pan, and fill baking dish with 3 cups boiling water.
7. Place the whole baking dish in the oven on the middle rack. Bake 20 minutes in the water bath, then reduce heat to 250°F and bake an additional 90 minutes, until the center is completely set.
8. Turn off oven and crack the door to allow the cake to cool slowly. Leave for about 1 hour (cooling the cake slowly prevents cracks on top of the cake). When the cake is cool enough to handle, remove it from the oven and top with the remaining caramel sauce.
9. Transfer the cake to the fridge and chill 6 hours (or overnight) to fully set.

WHITE CHOCOLATE RASPBERRY CHEESECAKE

 SERVES: 12-16   PREP: 7 HRS   COOK: 2 HRS

INGREDIENTS:

- 1 graham cracker crust (page 49)

Filling
- 1 cup cashews, soaked overnight
- ½ lb zucchini, peeled and chopped
- ½ cup honey
- ½ cup melted cacao butter
- ½ cup coconut cream
- ¼ cup lemon juice
- 1½ tsp apple cider vinegar
- 3 eggs
- 1 tbsp + 1 tsp vanilla
- 3 tbsp arrowroot starch
- 3 pints raspberries, divided

Glaze
- ½ pint raspberries
- ¼ cup water
- 1 tbsp honey
- 2 tsp lemon juice
- 1 tsp arrowroot starch + 1 tbsp water, mixed into a slurry

METHOD:

Prepare the filling:

1. Preheat the oven to 350°F.
2. Combine all filling ingredients in a high-powered blender or food processor and blend until smooth and creamy.
3. Spread 2 pints of raspberries in a single layer over the prepared crust. Reserve any extra raspberries for garnish.
4. Pour filling over raspberries in the crust.
5. Put the springform pan on a square of aluminum foil that's set in a baking dish. Fold the foil up to cover the sides of springform pan, and fill the baking dish with 3 cups boiling water.
6. Place the whole baking dish in the oven on the middle rack. Bake 20 minutes in water bath, then reduce heat to 250°F and bake an additional 90 minutes, until the center is completely set.
7. Turn off oven and crack the door to allow the cake to cool slowly. Leave for about 1 hour (cooling the cake slowly prevents cracks on top of the cake). When the cake is cool enough to handle, transfer it to the fridge and chill 6 hours (or overnight) to fully set.
8. Remove the cheesecake from the pan before glazing.

To make the glaze:

1. Simmer all ingredients (except arrowroot slurry) for 5 minutes, until raspberries dissolve.
2. Add arrowroot slurry and simmer another 2 minutes, to dissolve and thicken, whisking constantly.
3. Strain raspberry mixture through a mesh sieve and press through with the back of a spoon.
4. Pour glaze over prepared cheesecake, and top with remaining fresh raspberries.

CANDIED GINGER CHEESECAKE

SERVES: 12-16   **PREP: 7 HRS**   **COOK: 3 HRS**

INGREDIENTS:

Candied Ginger

- 2 cups water
- ½ lb ginger root, peeled and very thinly sliced
- 1¼ cups honey

Filling

- 1 cup cashews, soaked overnight
- ½ lb zucchini, peeled and chopped
- ½ cup ginger honey
- ½ cup coconut oil
- ⅔ cup coconut cream
- ¼ cup lemon juice
- 1½ tsp apple cider vinegar
- 3 eggs
- 2 tsp vanilla
- 3 tbsp arrowroot starch
- ¼ cup minced candied ginger

METHOD:

Prepare the candied ginger:

1. In a medium saucepan, bring water and ginger root to a boil, then cover and reduce to simmer 30 minutes.
2. Uncover and boil another 15 minutes.
3. Discard all but ¼ cup ginger water. Add honey to saucepan and simmer over low heat 30 minutes, stirring occasionally, until ginger is tender.
4. Strain candied ginger while honey is warm, and reserve the honey.

Prepare the filling:

1. Preheat the oven to 350°F.
2. Combine all ingredients except ginger in a high-powered blender or food processor and blend until smooth and creamy.
3. Add crystalized ginger to filling and blend.
4. Pour filling over prepared crust.
5. Put the springform pan on a square of aluminum foil, set in a baking dish. Fold the foil up to cover sides of springform pan, and fill baking dish with 3 cups boiling water.
6. Place the whole baking dish in the oven on middle rack. Bake 20 minutes, then reduce the heat to 250°F and bake an additional 90 minutes, until the center is completely set.
7. Turn off oven and crack the door to allow the cake to cool slowly. Leave for about 1 hour (cooling the cake slowly prevents cracks on top of the cake). When the cake is cool enough to handle, transfer it to the fridge and chill 6 hours (or overnight), to fully set.
8. To serve, top cheesecake with a spoonful or two of the ginger honey and some thinly sliced candied ginger.

LEMON BAR CHEESECAKE

SERVES: 12-16   **PREP: 7 HRS**   **COOK: 2 HRS**

INGREDIENTS:

Lemon Curd (page 40)

- ½ cup honey
- ⅓ cup fresh lemon juice
- 1 large egg
- 1 large egg yolk
- 1 tbsp collagen
- 3 tbsp coconut oil

Filling

- 1 cup cashews, soaked overnight
- ½ lb zucchini, peeled and chopped
- ½ cup honey
- ½ cup coconut oil
- ½ cup coconut cream
- ¼ cup lemon juice
- 1½ tsp apple cider vinegar
- 3 eggs
- 2 tsp vanilla

METHOD:

Prepare the lemon curd:

1. In a small saucepan, whisk together honey and lemon juice.
2. Heat mixture over medium until just simmering.
3. In a medium bowl, whisk eggs, collagen, and oil until they are smooth.
4. Slowly pour hot honey mixture into egg mixture, whisking constantly, to temper the eggs.
5. Return mixture to saucepan and heat on medium-low heat. Cook until thick, about 15 minutes, whisking constantly.
6. When lemon curd is thickened, transfer it to a container and press plastic wrap onto the top to prevent a film from forming. Allow the lemon curd to cool, then put the container in the fridge to set completely.

Tip: You can make the lemon curd 1-2 days ahead.

Prepare the filling:

1. Preheat the oven to 350°F.
2. Combine all ingredients except lemon curd in a high-powered blender or food processor and blend until smooth and creamy.
3. Pour filling over prepared crust. Using a spoon, dollop half the lemon curd into the batter and swirl it around (the lemon curd will sink, creating a really cool marbled effect in the cheesecake later).
4. Put the springform pan on a square of aluminum foil, set in a baking dish. Fold the foil up to cover sides of springform pan, and fill baking dish with 3 cups boiling water.
5. Place the whole baking dish in the oven on the middle rack. Bake 20 minutes, then reduce the heat to 250°F and bake an additional 90 minutes, until center is completely set.
6. Turn off oven and crack the door to allow the cake to cool slowly. Leave for about 1 hour (cooling the cake slowly prevents cracks on top of the cake). When the cake is cool enough to handle, remove it from the oven and top with the remaining lemon curd.
7. Transfer the cake to the fridge and chill 6 hours (or overnight) to fully set.

LAYERED MOCHA CHEESECAKE

🍴 SERVES: 12-16 🕐 PREP: 7 HRS 🕐 COOK: 2 HRS

INGREDIENTS:

Chocolate Graham Crust

- ¾ cup almond flour
- ½ cup arrowroot starch
- 3 tbsp cacao powder
- ½ tsp baking soda
- ¼ tsp salt
- ¼ cup coconut oil, melted
- 3 tbsp honey
- 1 tbsp molasses

Filling

- 1 cup cashews, soaked overnight
- ½ lb zucchini, peeled and chopped
- ½ cup honey
- ⅓ cup coconut oil
- ⅔ cup coconut cream
- ¼ cup lemon juice
- 1½ tsp apple cider vinegar
- 3 eggs
- 2 tsp vanilla
- ¼ tsp vanilla powder
- 3 tbsp arrowroot starch
- ¼ cup cacao powder
- 1¼ tsp ground decaf espresso

METHOD:

Prepare the chocolate graham crust:

1. Preheat the oven to 350°F.
2. Combine all ingredients in a medium bowl and mix to completely combine.
3. Press chocolate crust in a 7-inch or 8-inch springform pan.
4. Bake for 15 minutes, and allow to cool completely before pouring in the cheesecake filling.

Prepare the filling:

1. Preheat the oven to 350°F.
2. Blend all ingredients in a high powered blender except cacao and espresso.
3. Separate filling into 2 portions (about 2¼ cups each). Blend 1 portion with cacao. Whisk second portion with espresso.
4. Pour chocolate filling into the prepared crust and freeze until almost set, about 30 minutes.
5. Pour the espresso layer evenly over the chocolate layer.
6. Put the springform pan on a square of aluminum foil set in a baking dish. Fold the foil up to cover the sides of the springform pan, and fill the baking dish with 3 cups boiling water.
7. Place the whole baking dish in the oven on middle rack. Bake 20 minutes, then reduce the heat to 250°F and bake an additional 90 minutes, until center is completely set.
8. Turn off oven and crack the door to allow the cake to cool slowly. Leave for about 1 hour (cooling the cake is slowly prevents cracks on top of the cake). When the cake is cool enough to handle, remove it from the oven.
9. Top the cake with the chocolate ganache (page 23) and transfer the cake to the fridge and chill 6 hours-overnight, to fully set.
10. Heat a knife with hot water and use to cut before serving.

POMEGRANATE CHEESECAKE

SERVES: 12-16 **PREP: 7 HRS** **COOK: 2 HRS**

INGREDIENTS:

Filling

- 1 cup cashews, soaked overnight
- ½ lb zucchini, peeled and chopped
- ½ cup honey
- ⅓ cup coconut oil
- ⅔ cup coconut cream
- 3 tbsp reduced pomegranate juice*
- 1 tbsp lemon juice
- 2 tsp apple cider vinegar
- 3 eggs
- 2 tsp vanilla
- 3 tbsp arrowroot starch

Topping

- ¾ cup reduced pomegranate juice*
- 8 oz pomegranate seeds, about ½ a cup
- 2 tbsp honey
- 1 tbsp arrowroot starch

*Note: To reduce pomegranate juice, bring 2 cups juice to a boil over medium-high heat and boil 5-10 minutes until reduced by half. You should have 1 cup of reduced juice.

METHOD:

Prepare the filling:

1. Preheat the oven to 350°F.
2. Combine all ingredients in a high-powered blender or food processor and blend until smooth and creamy.
3. Pour filling over prepared crust.
4. Put the springform pan on a square of aluminum foil, set in a baking dish. Fold the foil up to cover the sides of the springform pan, and fill baking dish with 3 cups boiling water.
5. Place the whole baking dish in the oven on the middle rack. Bake 20 minutes, then reduce the heat to 250°F and bake an additional 90 minutes, until the center is completely set.
6. Turn off oven and crack the door to allow the cake to cool slowly. Leave for about 1 hour (cooling the cake slowly prevents cracks on top of the cake). When the cake is cool enough to handle, remove it from the oven, transfer it to the fridge and chill 6 hours (or overnight) to fully set.
7. Remove the cheesecake from the pan before topping with pomegranate sauce.

To prepare the topping:

1. Combine all ingredients in a small saucepan and whisk to completely combine.
2. Heat mixture over low, stirring constantly, until it just begins to thicken. At that point, remove it from the heat and allow it to cool.
3. Mix in the pomegranate seeds and pour the sauce over the cheesecake before slicing.

BLUEBERRY NO-BAKE CHEESECAKE

SERVES: 12-16   **PREP: 5 HRS**   **COOK: 0 MINS**

INGREDIENTS:

Crust

- 1 cup macadamia nuts or almonds
- 1 cup coconut, shredded
- ¼ tsp salt
- 1 cup dates
- 2 tbsp coconut oil

Filling

- 2 cups cashews, soaked overnight
- 1½ cups fresh blueberries
- ½ cup coconut oil
- ½ cup honey
- ½ cup coconut cream
- 3 tbsp lemon juice
- 1 tbsp vanilla

Topping

- ½ cup blueberries, plus more for garnish
- 2 tsp lemon juice
- 2 tbsp honey

METHOD:

Prepare the crust:

1. Line an 8-inch springform pan with parchment paper and set aside.

2. Process nuts into a flour in a food processor fitted with an "S" blade. Add coconut and salt and process again. Set aside.

3. Process dates and oil into a paste, then add nut mixture and coconut oil to date paste and process to form a crumbly but sticky dough.

4. Press dough into an even layer on the bottom of the prepared 8-inch springform pan.

5. Place crust in the fridge to set, 30 minutes (or overnight).

Prepare the filling:

1. Combine all ingredients in a high-powered blender and blend until smooth.

2. Pour filling over prepared crust. Transfer cake to the fridge to set, 4 hours (or overnight).

Prepare the topping:

1. Combine all ingredients in a blender and blend until smooth. Remove cake from the pan and pour topping over cake before serving.

pies

KEY LIME PIE

SERVES: 8-12   **PREP: 20 MINS**   **COOK: 20 MINS**

INGREDIENTS:

Graham Cracker Crust

- 1 batch graham crackers (page 91)
- 1 egg white

Filling

- 14.5 oz can full-fat coconut milk, divided
- 1 tbsp gelatin
- ¾ cup key lime juice
- ½ cup coconut cream
- ½ cup honey

METHOD:

Prepare the crust:

1. Preheat the oven to 350°F.

2. Break graham crackers into pieces and transfer to the bowl of a food processor fitted with an "S" blade. Process into a powder.

3. With the food processor still running, add egg white to graham crackers and process until a crumbly dough forms.

4. Dump the crumbly dough into a 9-inch pie pan and press it to line the pan in an even layer. Use a fork to poke holes in the bottom of the crust for even baking.

5. Bake crust 15-20 minutes, and allow to cool completely before filling.

Prepare the filling:

1. Pour ½ cup coconut milk into a medium mixing bowl and sprinkle gelatin over milk to hydrate.

2. In a small saucepan, bring key lime juice to a boil and reduce to ½ cup, about 5 minutes.

3. Add hot lime juice to gelatin and stir to dissolve.

4. Transfer all filling ingredients to a blender and blend until smooth. Pour filling into prepared graham cracker pie crust, and chill overnight to set.

5. Decorate pie with whipped cream and sliced limes before serving, if you like.

6. Store this pie in the fridge up to 4 days.

PERFECT PIE CRUST

SERVES: 8-12 **PREP: 50 MINS** **COOK: 20 MINS**

INGREDIENTS:

- ½ cup almond flour
- ½ cup arrowroot starch
- ½ cup coconut flour
- ¼ tsp salt
- ½ cup palm shortening
- ¼ cup water

METHOD:

To prepare the dough:

1. Combine almond flour, arrowroot, coconut flour, and salt in a medium bowl, and mix to completely combine.

2. Cut in palm shortening to form a crumbly dough.

3. Add the water to the crumbly dough and mix until a smooth dough forms. If the dough is still crumbly, add water 1 tablespoon at a time until a smooth dough is formed.

4. Form the dough into a ball, wrap it in plastic wrap, and refrigerate 30 minutes (or overnight).

To bake the crust:

1. Preheat the oven to 350°F.

2. Remove dough from the fridge and allow it to sit out 10-15 minutes. This will make it easier to roll.

3. When dough is ready, unwrap and place it between two pieces of parchment paper. Press dough down slightly, and then use a rolling pin to roll dough into a ¼-inch thick circle. Remove the top sheet of parchment paper and smooth the edges to even them out.

4. Place a 9-inch pie pan upside down on top of the dough. Carefully turn dough and pie pan right-side up, so dough is resting in the pie pan and the sheet of parchment paper is on top. Carefully press dough into the pie pan and gently remove parchment paper.

5. Use your fingers to even out the edges and smooth the cracks, until the pie crust is formed in the pan. Use a fork to poke holes in the bottom of the crust for even baking.

6. Bake crust 20 minutes, until firm to the touch and very lightly golden on the edges.

7. Allow crust to cool completely before filling.

BANOFFEE PIE

🍴 SERVES: 8-12 🕐 PREP: 2 HRS 🕐 COOK: 0 MINS

INGREDIENTS:

- 1 9-inch prebaked pie crust (page 69)

Whipped Cream

- ½ cup water, divided
- 2 tsp gelatin
- 1½ cup coconut cream
- 2 tbsp honey
- 1 tsp vanilla

Toffee Filling

- 1 cup ghee
- 1 cup coconut sugar
- 1 tsp vanilla
- 3 tbsp coconut cream
- 2 tbsp coconut oil

Pie

- 2-3 large, ripe bananas, sliced into rounds
- Unsweetened baking chocolate, shaved, to decorate (optional)

METHOD:

To prepare the whipped cream:

1. Pour ¼ cup water into a medium bowl. Sprinkle gelatin evenly over water to allow it to "hydrate."

2. Once gelatin has hydrated, add ¼ cup boiling water and stir to dissolve gelatin. Add coconut cream, honey, and vanilla to the bowl and use an electric mixer or a whisk to whip ingredients together.

3. Set whipped cream in the fridge to set, about 30 minutes.

4. While the whipped cream is setting, prepare the toffee.

Tip: You can prepare the whipped cream a day in advance.

To prepare the toffee:

1. In a medium saucepan, heat ghee over medium-low heat until melted.

2. Add coconut sugar, vanilla, coconut cream, and oil and whisk to dissolve sugar. Continue cooking to allow the toffee to thicken, stirring constantly, about 5 minutes.

3. Set the toffee aside to cool.

To assemble the pie:

1. Pour ½ the toffee into the prepared pie crust.

2. Top with ⅔ of the sliced bananas.

3. Top with remaining toffee and smooth to cover all bananas.

4. Place pie in the fridge to allow toffee to set, 1 hour.

5. When toffee is set, top pie with whipped cream. Decorate with remaining sliced bananas and shaved chocolate, if you like.

6. Store the pie covered in the fridge up to 3 days.

PEACH MELBA PIE

🍴 **SERVES: 8-12** 🕐 **PREP: 20 MINS** 🕐 **COOK: 1 HR 20 MINS**

INGREDIENTS:

- 1 9-inch prebaked pie crust (page 69)
- 5 cups chopped peaches, fresh, peeled (make sure they're ripe)
- 6 oz raspberries
- ½ cup almond flour
- ¼ tsp salt
- 1 tbsp honey
- 2 tbsp coconut oil
- ½ tsp vanilla
- ¼ cup reserved juices from the peaches (or available reserved juices + water to = ¼ c)
- 1 tbsp fruity white wine, such as sauvignon blanc, OR lemon juice
- 2 tbsp arrowroot
- 2 tbsp honey

METHOD:

To prepare the peaches:

1. Bring a large pot of water to boil. Prepare a large bowl of ice water and set aside.
2. Pierce the bottom of each peach with a sharp knife, making a small "X."
3. Place peaches in boiling water and boil for 2-3 minutes, then remove from boiling water and place in ice water. Allow peaches to cool, then remove from ice water and peel off the skin.
4. Cut peeled peaches away from the pit, chop them, and place in a large bowl to allow the juices to collect.
5. Strain juices into a small bowl, and add raspberries.

To prepare the pie:

1. Preheat the oven to 375°F.
2. In a small bowl, combine almond flour, salt, honey, coconut oil, and vanilla and mix to completely combine. Set the mixture aside.
3. In a small saucepan combine reserved peach juices, wine, and arrowroot and whisk to make a slurry. Add honey and stir to combine.
4. Turn the heat up to low-medium and allow the slurry to thicken, whisking constantly, about 3-5 minutes.
5. Just as the slurry begins to thicken, remove the pot from heat and pour the slurry over the peaches and raspberries. Mix well to coat fruit in the slurry.
6. Pour peaches into prepared pie crust, and sprinkle crumble mixture evenly over the fruit.
7. Bake the pie for 20 minutes at 375°F, then reduce heat to 350°F and continue baking 60 minutes longer, until the crumble topping is browned and the filling is bubbling.
8. Remove the pie from the oven and allow it to cool completely before serving.
9. Store this pie covered in the fridge up to 3 days.

LEMON MERINGUE PIE

SERVES: 8-12 **PREP: 25 MINS** **COOK: 15 MINS**

INGREDIENTS:

- 1 prebaked pie crust (page 69)

Filling

- 2 whole eggs
- 4 egg yolks (whites reserved for topping)
- 3 tbsp arrowroot starch, divided
- 4 egg whites
- ½ tsp cream of tartar
- 2 tbsp maple syrup
- ½ tsp vanilla
- 1 tbsp boiling water
- Pinch of salt
- ½ cup + 2 tbsp lemon juice
- Zest of 1 medium lemon
- ½ cup water
- ½ cup honey

METHOD:

1. Preheat the oven to 375°F.

2. Whisk together eggs, yolks and 2 tbsp arrowroot in a medium bowl and set aside.

3. In a large bowl, combine egg whites and cream of tartar. Set aside.

4. In a small bowl, whisk remaining arrowroot with maple syrup and vanilla to form a smooth paste. Add boiling water and salt and whisk to combine.

5. Using an electric mixer, beat egg whites on medium speed until they become foamy. Add maple syrup mixture and continue beating until it becomes glossy and forms stiff peaks, about 10 minutes. Set aside.

6. Heat lemon juice, zest, water, and honey in a small saucepan.

7. Slowly pour heated lemon juice blend into the yolk mixture, whisking constantly, until smooth.

8. Return the egg-lemon juice mixture to the saucepan and heat over low. Whisk constantly until the mixture just begins to thicken. Remove it from the heat and pour the mixture into the pie crust.

9. Top lemon filling with whipped egg whites, making sure the meringue reaches the edges of the pie. Using the back of a spoon, make peaks and points over the top of the pie.

10. Bake for 10-15 minutes, until the meringue is golden. Cool completely before cutting and serving.

11. Store the pie covered in the fridge for 3-4 days.

CHOCOLATE PUDDING PIE

🍴 SERVES: 8-12   🕐 PREP: 5 HRS 30 MINS   🕐 COOK: 20 MINS

INGREDIENTS:

Crust

- 1 recipe Oreo cookies (no filling), finely crushed (page 108)
- 2 egg whites

Filling

- ⅓ cup water
- 1 tbsp gelatin
- 14.5 oz full-fat coconut milk
- ⅓ cup maple syrup
- ⅓ cup cacao powder
- 1 tsp vanilla

Whipped Topping

- 1½ cup coconut cream
- ¼ cup maple syrup
- 1 tsp vanilla
- ½ cup water, divided
- 2 tsp gelatin
- Shaved chocolate, optional, to decorate

METHOD:

To prepare the crust:

1. Preheat the oven to 350°F.
2. Transfer cookies to the bowl of a food processor fitted with an "S" blade. Process the cookies into a powder.
3. With the food processor still running, add egg whites to the powdered cookies and process until a crumbly dough forms.
4. Dump crumbly dough into a 9-inch pie pan and press it to line the pan in an even layer. Use a fork to poke holes in the bottom of the crust for even baking.
5. Bake crust 15-20 minutes, and allow it to cool completely before filling.

To prepare the filling:

1. Pour water into a medium bowl and sprinkle gelatin over it to hydrate.
2. While gelatin is hydrating, bring coconut milk to a boil in a small saucepan.
3. Pour hot coconut milk over gelatin and stir well to dissolve.
4. In a small bowl, combine maple syrup and cacao and whisk until smooth.
5. Add the cacao-maple syrup mixture and vanilla to coconut milk and whisk to combine.

6. Allow filling to cool completely before pouring into the pie shell.

7. Transfer pie to the fridge to allow filling to set until firm, about 4 hours (or overnight).

To prepare the whipped topping:

1. Combine coconut cream, maple syrup, and vanilla in a medium bowl and mix well. Set aside.

2. In a small bowl, add ¼ cup cool water and sprinkle gelatin over water to allow it to hydrate. While gelatin is hydrating bring ¼ cup water to a boil.

3. When gelatin is hydrated, pour boiling water over it and stir to dissolve.

4. Add dissolved gelatin to coconut cream mixture and whip to combine.

5. Place whipped topping in the fridge to chill and set, 1 hour (or overnight).

To assemble:

1. When whipped topping is set, whisk it to make it fluffy again and spread it over the pie filling.

2. Place the pie in the fridge to set for about 30 minutes. Decorate pie with shaved dark chocolate if you like.

3. Store the pie covered in the fridge up to 4 days.

Tip: The components of this pie can all be made 1-2 days ahead of time, and then assembled the day of serving.

PECAN PIE

SERVES: 8-12   **PREP: 5 MINS**   **COOK: 30 MINS**

INGREDIENTS:

- 1 9-inch prebaked pie crust (page 69)
- ½ cup pure maple syrup
- 2 tbsp coconut sugar
- 2 tbsp molasses
- 2 eggs
- 1 tsp vanilla
- ¼ tsp lemon juice
- 2 tbsp coconut oil
- 1½ cup chopped pecans
- ¼ cup pecan halves (to decorate)

METHOD:

1. Preheat the oven to 375°F.

2. Combine all ingredients except pecans in a medium bowl and stir well to completely combine.

3. Add chopped pecans and mix well.

4. Pour filling into prepared pie crust, and use pecan halves to decorate the top of the pie.

5. Bake 25-30 minutes, until middle of the pie is set and no longer jiggly.

6. Allow pie to cool completely before serving.

BLUEBERRY CREAM TART

SERVES: 8-12　　**PREP: 4 HRS 40 MINS**　　**COOK: 1 HR**

INGREDIENTS:

- 1 prebaked crust (page 69) prepared in tart pan
- 4 eggs
- ¼ cup arrowroot starch
- ⅓ cup honey
- Pinch of salt
- 1½ tsp vanilla
- 14.5 oz can full-fat coconut milk
- 1½ cups fresh blueberries

METHOD:

1. Create an ice bath by filling a large bowl ¼ of the way full with ice, then add water to fill the bowl about halfway. Set aside.

2. In a medium bowl combine eggs, arrowroot, honey, salt, and vanilla. Whisk until smooth.

3. In a medium saucepan heat coconut milk until just simmering.

4. Slowly pour hot coconut milk into egg mixture, whisking constantly, to temper the eggs.

5. Return mixture to saucepan and heat over low, whisking constantly, until mixture begins to thicken, about 10-20 minutes.

6. Once mixture has thickened, return it to the mixing bowl, and place mixing bowl in the ice bath to cool.

7. While the mixture is cooling, preheat the oven to 325°F.

8. When the mixture is cooled, pour into prepared tart crust and sprinkle blueberries in an even layer over the top.

9. Bake tart until set and the center is no longer jiggly, 50-60 minutes.

10. Remove tart from the oven and allow it to cool completely, then chill 4 hours (or overnight) to set before serving.

APPLE GALETTE

🍴 SERVES: 8-12 🕐 PREP: 25 MINS 🕐 COOK: 55 MINS

INGREDIENTS:

- 4 golden delicious apples
- 1 tbsp lemon juice
- 1 batch pie dough, unbaked (page 69)
- 5 tbsp ghee, divided
- 3 tbsp honey
- 1 tsp cinnamon

METHOD:

1. Preheat the oven to 400°F. Line a baking sheet with parchment paper or silpat and set aside.

2. Peel and halve the apples, then cut out cores. Slice apples into ¼ inch slices. Put apples in a medium bowl and toss with lemon juice. Set aside.

3. Roll out pie dough between two pieces of parchment paper into a large circle, about ¼-inch thick.

4. In a small saucepan, melt 3 tablespoons of ghee with honey. Add cinnamon and mix.

5. Remove honey ghee from heat and use a pastry brush or BBQ brush to brush dough with honey ghee.

6. Arrange half of the apple slices in a single, circular layer over dough, leaving a 2-inch edge. Brush apples with honey ghee. Finish with a second layer of the remaining apple slices, and drizzle the remaining honey ghee over all apples. Carefully use the edges of the parchment paper to help you fold the edges of the crust just over the edge of the apples.

7. Melt the remaining 2 tablespoons ghee in the small saucepan and brush the top of apples and crust with ghee.

8. Bake galette 25 minutes, then reduce heat to 350°F. Again, brush apples and crust with ghee, and bake another 30 minutes, until apples are tender and crust is golden.

9. Serve warm or room temperature.

CHERRY PIE

SERVES: 8-12 · **PREP: 10 MINS** · **COOK: 1 HR**

INGREDIENTS:

- 2 pie crust recipes, separated into 2 equal portions (page 69)
- 5 cups canned tart cherries, well drained
- ½ cup reserved cherry juice
- 4 tbsp arrowroot starch
- ¼ cup honey
- ½ cup coconut sugar

METHOD:

1. Preheat the oven to 350°F.

2. Roll out both portions of pie dough into ¼-inch thick circles. Press one of the circles into the pie pan and bake as normal. Set the other dough circle aside.

3. Place cherries in a large bowl and set aside.

4. In a small saucepan, combine reserved cherry juices and arrowroot and whisk to combine. Add honey and sugar and heat over low, stirring constantly, until mixture just begins to thicken.

5. Remove mixture from heat and pour it over cherries. Stir to completely cover cherries.

6. Pour cherry mixture into the bottom pie crust. Carefully add the top pie crust and pinch the edges together with the bottom crust. Smooth out any cracks by dipping your fingertip in water, then gently massaging the crack back together.

7. Use a sharp knife to pierce holes in the middle of the top crust to let the steam escape.

8. Place the pie on a baking sheet on the center rack of the oven for 45-60 minutes.

9. Remove pie from the oven and allow it to cool completely before serving.

10. Store pie covered in the fridge, for up to 3 days.

FRENCH COCONUT PIE

🍴 SERVES: 8-12 ⏱ PREP: 5 MINS ⏱ COOK: 45 MINS

INGREDIENTS:

- 9-inch prebaked pie crust (page 69)
- 3 large eggs
- 14.5 oz can full-fat coconut milk
- 1 tbsp lemon juice
- 3 tbsp arrowroot starch
- ⅓ cup coconut oil, melted
- 1 tsp vanilla
- ½ cup honey
- 1½ cup shredded coconut

METHOD:

1. Preheat the oven to 350°F.

2. Combine all ingredients in a large mixing bowl and whisk until completely combined.

3. Pour filling into prepared pie crust and bake 40-45 minutes, until the edges of the filling are golden brown and the center isn't jiggly when lightly shaken.

4. Remove pie from the oven and allow it to cool completely before serving.

5. Store pie covered in the fridge up to 3 days.

STRAWBERRY ICEBOX PIE

🍴 SERVES: 8-12   🕐 PREP: 4 HRS 30 MINS   🕐 COOK: 0 MINS

INGREDIENTS:

- 1 9-inch prebaked pie crust (page 69)
- ¼ cup lemon juice
- 4 tsp gelatin
- 4 tbsp boiling water
- 4 cups fresh strawberries + 1 cup for garnish
- ⅓ cup honey

METHOD:

1. Pour lemon juice into a small bowl, and sprinkle gelatin over it to hydrate.

2. While gelatin is hydrating, bring water to a boil in a medium saucepan.

3. Add hot water to hydrated gelatin and stir to dissolve.

4. Add 4 cups strawberries and honey to the saucepan and bring everything to a boil. Reduce heat to a simmer and cook for 10 minutes, until strawberries are soft. When the strawberries are softened, add the lemon juice-gelatin mixture and stir to combine. Set the filling aside to cool slightly, about 10 minutes.

5. Pour strawberry filling into prepared pie shell, and finish the pie by arranging the remaining 1 cup whole strawberries on top.

6. Transfer pie to the fridge and allow it to chill to set, 4 hours (or overnight).

7. Serve cold and enjoy!

cookies

SNICKERDOODLES

YIELDS: 12 · **PREP: 10 MINS** · **COOK: 20 MINS**

INGREDIENTS:

- 2 tbsp cinnamon
- 1 egg
- ½ cup coconut sugar
- 1 cup almond flour
- 1 tsp cream of tartar
- ½ cup arrowroot starch
- ½ tsp baking soda
- ¼ tsp salt
- ¼ cup palm shortening, softened to room temperature

METHOD:

1. Preheat the oven to 350°F. Line a baking sheet with parchment paper or silpat and set aside.

2. Place cinnamon in a small bowl and set aside.

3. Combine egg and sugar in a small bowl and mix to dissolve sugar.

4. In a medium bowl combine almond flour, cream of tartar, arrowroot, baking soda, and salt, and mix to completely combine.

5. Add egg-sugar mixture to almond flour mixture and stir well until a thick batter is formed.

6. Mix in shortening until completely combined.

7. Using a tablespoon or medium/#40 cookie scoop, scoop dough and drop it into the bowl of cinnamon. Using a fork, flip dough to completely cover it in cinnamon, then transfer it to prepared baking sheet.

8. Repeat with remaining dough, leaving 2 inches of space between each portion on the baking sheet (they will spread).

9. Bake for 15-20 minutes until edges of cookies are golden brown.

10. When the cookies are finished baking, remove from oven and allow to cool slightly before transferring to a wire rack to finish cooling.

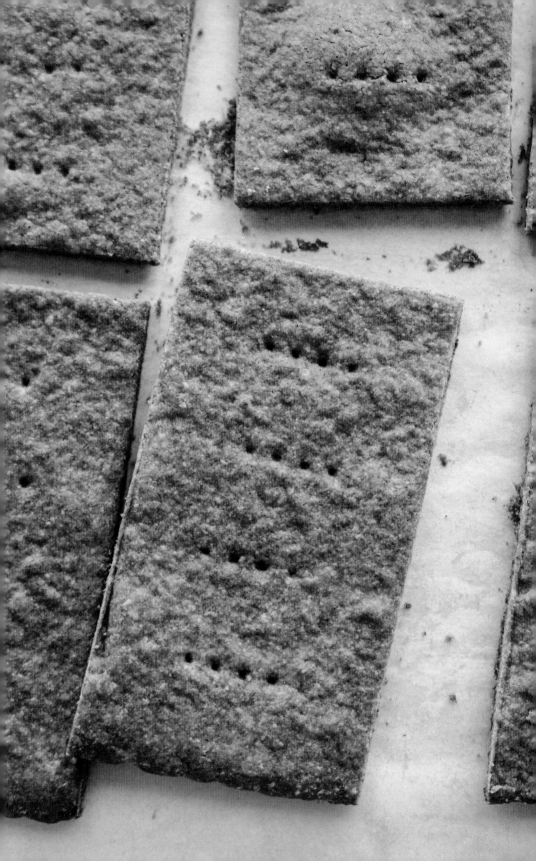

GRAHAM CRACKERS

SERVES: 8-10 · **PREP: 10 MINS** · **COOK: 12 MINS**

INGREDIENTS:

- ¾ cup almond flour
- ½ cup arrowroot starch
- 1 tbsp coconut flour
- ½ tsp baking soda
- ¼ tsp salt
- ¼ cup melted coconut oil
- 3 tbsp honey
- 1 tbsp molasses

METHOD:

1. Preheat the oven to 350°F.

2. Combine almond flour, arrowroot, coconut flour, baking soda, and salt in a medium mixing bowl. Whisk to completely incorporate.

3. Add coconut oil, honey, and molasses to the center of the bowl and whisk them together as you mix to form a dough.

4. Roll out dough between 2 pieces of parchment paper until about ⅛ inch to ¼ inch thick, shaping into a rectangle as you work.

5. Peel off top piece of parchment paper and transfer flattened dough rectangle onto a baking sheet.

6. Carefully cut dough into smaller rectangular crackers, and pierce each rectangle with a fork several times.

7. Bake for 10-12 minutes, until crackers are golden and darkened around the edges.

8. When crackers are done baking, remove from the oven and cut dough once again along the same lines.

9. Transfer crackers to a wire rack to finish cooling. Break apart, and enjoy!

LOFTHOUSE SUGAR COOKIES

🍴 YIELDS: 12 🕐 PREP: 1 HR 10 MINS 🕐 COOK: 20 MINS

INGREDIENTS:

- 1 cup almond flour
- ½ cup arrowroot starch
- ½ tsp baking soda
- ¼ tsp salt
- 1 egg
- ½ cup coconut sugar
- 1 tsp vanilla extract
- ¼ cup palm shortening, softened to room temperature

METHOD:

Prepare the dough:

1. Combine almond flour, arrowroot, baking soda, and salt in a medium mixing bowl and mix well.

2. In a small bowl whisk egg with sugar and vanilla until well mixed.

3. Add egg to almond flour mixture and stir well.

4. Add shortening to dough and mix well to completely incorporate.

5. Turn dough out onto a piece of parchment paper and form into a 2-inch to 3-inch wide log. Roll the log up in the parchment paper and place it in the freezer to set 1 hour (or overnight).

To bake:

1. Preheat the oven to 350°F. Line a baking sheet with parchment paper or silpat and set aside.

2. Remove dough from freezer and use a sharp knife to slice into ¼-inch thick rounds. Arrange on prepared baking sheet with 2 inches between each cookie (they will spread).

3. Bake 15-20 minutes until browned around the edges.

4. Allow cookies to cool completely before serving.

CUT-OUT SUGAR COOKIES

🍴 YIELDS: 12-14   🕐 PREP: 55 MINS   🕐 COOK: 12 MINS

INGREDIENTS:

- ¾ cup almond flour
- ⅓ cup arrowroot starch + 4 tbsp
- 1 tbsp coconut flour
- ½ tsp baking soda
- ¼ tsp salt
- ¼ cup melted coconut oil
- ¼ cup maple syrup
- 2 tsp vanilla

METHOD:

To prepare the cookie dough:

1. Combine almond flour, arrowroot, coconut flour, baking soda, and salt in a medium mixing bowl. Stir well to completely combine.

2. In a small bowl mix oil, maple syrup, and vanilla until well mixed.

3. Add oil mixture to almond flour mixture and stir well to completely combine.

4. Roll out dough into a ¼-inch circle between two pieces of parchment paper.

5. Place rolled dough in the freezer for 30 minutes to set.

To bake the cookies:

1. Preheat the oven to 350°F. Line a baking sheet with parchment paper or silpat and set aside.

2. When dough is set, remove from freezer and work quickly using cookie cutters to cut out shapes. Use a spatula to transfer shapes to the prepared baking sheet.

3. Re-roll dough scraps into a ¼-inch round, and re-freeze dough about 10-15 minutes. Repeat cutting process with remaining dough.

4. When the cookies are ready, place baking sheet in the oven and bake 10-12 minutes, until cookies are golden around the edges.

5. Allow cookies to cool fully before serving.

Tip: If the cookies go soft, place them in a single layer on a baking sheet and bake for 5 minutes at 300°F. Allow them to cool fully before serving.

GLUTEN-FREE VEGAN CHOCOLATE CHIP COOKIES

YIELDS: 12-14 · **PREP: 5 MINS** · **COOK: 15 MINS**

INGREDIENTS:

- 1½ cups almond flour
- 2 tbsp arrowroot starch
- ¼ tsp sea salt
- ½ tsp baking soda
- 2 tsp vanilla
- ⅓ cup maple syrup
- ¼ cup ghee or coconut oil, melted
- ⅓ cup chocolate chunks (see recipe for chocolate chunks in Chocolate Chip Cookie Cake, page 32)

METHOD:

1. Preheat the oven to 350°F. Line a baking sheet with parchment paper or silpat and set aside.

2. In a medium bowl combine almond flour, arrowroot, salt, and baking soda. Mix to combine.

3. Combine vanilla, maple syrup, and ghee in a small bowl and mix.

4. Add maple syrup mixture to almond flour mixture and stir well until completely combined.

5. Fold in chocolate chunks.

6. Use a tablespoon or medium/#40 cookie scoop to portion dough onto prepared baking sheet, leaving 2 inches of space between each portion.

7. Bake 10-15 minutes, until cookies are golden brown around the edges. They will be lighter in color than regular chocolate chip cookies.

8. Remove cookies from oven and allow them to cool slightly before moving to a wire rack to finish cooling.

LAVENDER SHORTBREAD COOKIES

🍴 **YIELDS: 20-24**   🕐 **PREP: 1 HR 10 MINS**   🕐 **COOK: 30 MINS**

INGREDIENTS:

- ½ cup coconut flour
- ½ cup arrowroot powder
- ¼ tsp salt
- 2½ tsp dried lavender flowers, finely minced
- ¼ cup ghee, softened to room temperature
- 1 egg white
- 3 tbsp honey
- ½ tsp vanilla

METHOD:

To prepare the dough:

1. Add coconut flour, arrowroot, salt, lavender, and ghee to the bowl of a food processor fitted with an "S" blade, and process into a crumbly dough.

2. With food processor running, add egg white, honey, and vanilla, and continue to process until a crumbly dough is formed again.

3. Scoop by tablespoonful into cups of a muffin tin and press dough down to fill in any cracks (a silicone muffin form works best for this). Alternatively, you can simply roll dough into a 2-inch log on a piece of parchment paper, and wrap it up in the parchment paper.

4. Place dough in the fridge 1 hour (or overnight).

To bake the cookies:

1. Preheat the oven to 325°F. Line a baking sheet with parchment paper or silpat and set aside.

2. If you used a muffin tin to shape the dough, turn dough out onto prepared baking sheet.

3. If you rolled the dough into a log, unwrap dough from parchment paper and use a sharp knife to slice into ¼-inch rounds. Arrange rounds on prepared baking sheet.

4. Bake for 25-30 minutes, until the edges of the cookies are golden brown and firm to the touch.

5. Allow cookies to cool completely before serving, to ensure they're as crispy as possible.

CINNAMON RAISIN ALMOND COOKIES

YIELDS: 12-14 **PREP: 10 MINS** **COOK: 15 MINS**

INGREDIENTS:

- 1½ cup almond flour
- ¼ tsp sea salt
- 2 tsp cinnamon
- ½ tsp baking soda
- 2 tsp vanilla
- ⅓ cup maple syrup
- ¼ cup ghee or coconut oil, melted
- ¼ cup raisins
- ¼ cup sliced almonds

METHOD:

1. Preheat the oven to 350°F. Line a baking sheet with parchment paper or silpat and set aside.

2. In a medium bowl combine almond flour, salt, cinnamon, and baking soda. Mix to combine.

3. Combine vanilla, maple syrup, and ghee in a small bowl and mix.

4. Add maple syrup mixture to almond flour mixture and stir well until completely combined.

5. Fold in raisins and sliced almonds.

6. Use a tablespoon or medium/#40 cookie scoop to portion dough onto prepared baking sheet, leaving 2 inches of space between each portion.

7. Bake 15 minutes, until cookies are golden brown around the edges.

8. Remove cookies and allow to cool slightly before moving to a wire rack to finish cooling.

ORANGE WALNUT CRANBERRY COOKIES

YIELDS: 12-14 · PREP: 10 MINS · COOK: 15 MINS

INGREDIENTS:

- ½ cup almond flour
- 1 cup walnut flour
- 3 tbsp arrowroot
- ¼ tsp sea salt
- ½ tsp baking soda
- 1 tsp vanilla
- 1½ tsp fresh grated orange zest
- ⅓ cup maple syrup
- ¼ cup ghee or coconut oil, melted
- ⅓ cup dried cranberries

METHOD:

1. Preheat the oven to 350°F. Line a baking sheet with parchment paper or silpat and set aside.

2. In a medium bowl combine flours, arrowroot, salt, and baking soda. Mix to combine.

3. In a small bowl combine vanilla, orange zest, maple syrup, and ghee and mix.

4. Add maple syrup mixture to almond flour mixture and stir well until completely combined.

5. Fold in cranberries.

6. Use a tablespoon or medium/#40 cookie scoop to portion dough onto prepared baking sheet, leaving 2 inches of space between each portion.

7. Bake 15 minutes, until cookies are golden brown around the edges.

8. Remove cookies and allow to cool slightly before moving to a wire rack to finish cooling.

Tip: To make walnut flour, process 1¼ cups walnuts in a food processor until they are finely ground.

SLICE-N-BAKE
BROWNIE COOKIES

YIELDS: 12-15   **PREP: 2 HRS 10 MINS**   **COOK: 15 MINS**

INGREDIENTS:

- 1 cup raw almond butter*
- 1 tsp vanilla
- 2 eggs
- ⅔ cup coconut sugar
- 3 tbsp cacao powder
- ½ tsp baking soda
- ¼ tsp salt
- ¼ cup chopped walnuts, toasted

*The oil in raw almond butter is different than the oil found in roasted almond butter—this yields a different texture in the cookie.

METHOD:

To prepare the dough:

1. In a medium mixing bowl, combine almond butter and vanilla.
2. In a small bowl, combine eggs and sugar and stir well to dissolve sugar.
3. In a separate small bowl combine cacao, baking soda, and salt, and whisk together.
4. Add sugar-egg mixture to almond butter and mix to form a smooth paste.
5. Add cacao mixture to almond butter mixture and stir to completely combine.
6. Fold in walnuts.
7. Place dough on a piece of parchment paper and roll into a log. Freeze dough 2 hours to set, or keep up to 3 weeks.

To bake the cookies:

1. Preheat the oven to 350°F. Line a baking sheet with parchment paper or silpat and set aside.
2. Remove dough from freezer, unwrap, and use a sharp knife to cut into ¼-inch rounds. Place rounds on prepared baking sheet with 2 inches between them.
3. Bake 15-18 minutes, until cookies are set and slightly darker brown around the edges.
4. Remove cookies from heat and allow to cool on a wire rack before serving.

LEMON SQUARES

YIELDS: 12-16   **PREP:** 1 HRS 10 MINS   **COOK:** 55 MINS

INGREDIENTS:

- 1 pie crust, unbaked (page 69)

Filling

- ½ cup applesauce
- ½ cup honey
- ½ cup lemon juice
- 1 tbsp coconut flour
- 5 large eggs

METHOD:

1. Preheat the oven to 350°F.
2. Line an 8x8x2-inch baking dish with parchment paper.
3. Place dough in parchment lined dish and press to cover bottom of dish in an even layer.
4. Bake crust until just golden brown, 20-25 minutes. Remove from oven and allow to cool completely before adding filling.

To prepare the filling:

1. Combine all ingredients in a medium bowl and whisk well to completely combine. The mixture will not be perfectly smooth because of the applesauce, but it should be completely incorporated.
2. Pour filling into prepared crust and bake 25-30 minutes, until the center is set and does not jiggle when lightly shaken.
3. Remove bars from oven and allow to cool completely. Transfer to fridge and let chill to set 1 hour (or overnight) before serving.

PALEO OREOS

SERVES: 10-12 **PREP: 40 MINS** **COOK: 12 MINS**

INGREDIENTS:

Chocolate Cookie

- ¾ cup almond flour
- ⅓ cup arrowroot starch
- ¼ cup cacao powder
- ½ tsp baking soda
- ¼ tsp salt
- ¼ cup coconut oil, melted
- ¼ cup maple syrup
- 1 tsp vanilla

Filling

- 2 tbsp honey
- ½ tsp vanilla
- 2 grams powdered stevia
- 3 tbsp arrowroot starch
- ½ cup palm shortening

METHOD:

Prepare the dough:

1. Combine almond flour, arrowroot, cacao, baking soda, and salt in a medium mixing bowl.

2. In a small mixing bowl, combine oil, maple syrup, and vanilla, and whisk to combine.

3. Add oil mixture to almond flour mixture and combine to form a dough.

4. Scoop dough onto a sheet of parchment paper and form into a log. Roll up the log in the parchment paper and put in the freezer to set, about 30 minutes.

To prepare the filling:

1. In a medium bowl, whisk honey, vanilla, stevia, and arrowroot into a smooth paste.

2. Add shortening and use an electric mixer or whisk to whip the frosting together, and then set aside.

To bake the cookie:

1. Preheat the oven to 350°F.

2. Remove cookie dough from the freezer and unwrap it.

3. Use a sharp knife to cut dough into 24 thin rounds, about ⅛-inch thick, and place them on a parchment-lined or silpat-lined baking sheet.

4. Bake cookies for 10-12 minutes, until crispy and darkened around the edges.

5. Remove cookies from the oven and allow to cool slightly on the baking sheet before transferring to a wire rack to finish cooling.

To assemble the cookies:

1. Scoop 1 teaspoon of filling onto a cookie, and top with another cookie to create a sandwich.

2. Repeat with remaining cookies.

Tip: You can place the prepared cookies in the fridge to set the filling faster.

ice cream

1. Chai Spice-Cream
2. Honey Vanilla Ice Cream
3. Mint Chocolate Chip Ice Cream
4. Banana Split Ice Cream
5. Salted Chocolate Ice Cream with Toasted Almonds & Cacao Nibs
6. Salted Caramel Ice Cream
7. Balsamic Roasted Strawberry Ice Cream
9. Lemon Chiffon Ice Cream
8. S'mores Ice Cream
10. No-Churn Avocado Ice Cream

CHAI SPICE-CREAM

SERVES: 4-6 **PREP: OVERNIGHT + 3 HRS 30 MINS** **COOK: 0 MINS**

INGREDIENTS:

- 14.5 oz can full-fat coconut milk
- 2 bags rooibos chai tea
- 3 egg yolks
- ⅛ tsp cinnamon
- ⅛ tsp ginger
- ⅛ tsp ground black pepper
- ½ cup maple syrup
- 1 tsp vanilla
- ⅛ tsp salt

METHOD:

1. In a small saucepan bring milk to a boil.

2. Turn off heat and add tea bags. Let milk cool completely, then transfer mixture to fridge to steep overnight.

3. Place egg yolks, spices, and maple syrup in a medium mixing bowl and whisk until smooth. Set aside.

4. Heat infused milk over medium heat in a small saucepan until just simmering.

5. Slowly pour hot milk into egg mixture, whisking constantly, to temper eggs.

6. When all milk is whisked in, transfer mixture back to saucepan and return to low heat.

7. Continue whisking until mixture thickens into a custard-like consistency, about 15-20 minutes. Whisk in vanilla and salt.

8. Once mixture has thickened, remove from heat and pour into a small bowl or desired container. Allow mixture to cool completely, then transfer to fridge to chill 2 hours (or overnight).

9. Once mixture has cooled, pour into ice cream maker and process according to instructions on the machine.

10. Transfer ice cream back to container and store in freezer. Allow it to freeze 1 hour (or overnight) before serving.

HONEY VANILLA ICE CREAM

🍴 SERVES: 4-6 🕐 PREP: 3 HRS 30 MINS 🕐 COOK: 0 MINS

INGREDIENTS:

- 3 egg yolks
- ½ cup creamed honey
- 14.5 oz can full-fat coconut milk
- 2 tsp vanilla
- ⅛ tsp salt

METHOD:

1. Place egg yolks and honey in a medium mixing bowl and whisk until smooth. Set aside.

2. Heat milk over medium heat in a small saucepan until just simmering.

3. Slowly pour hot milk into egg mixture, whisking constantly to temper the eggs.

4. When all milk is whisked in, transfer mixture back to saucepan and return to low heat.

5. Continue whisking until mixture thickens into a custard-like consistency, about 15-20 minutes. Whisk in vanilla and salt.

6. Once mixture has thickened, remove from heat and pour into a small bowl or desired container. Allow mixture to cool completely, then transfer to fridge to chill 2 hours (or overnight).

7. Once mixture has cooled, pour into ice cream maker and process according to the instructions on the machine.

8. Transfer ice cream back to container and store in freezer. Allow to freeze 1 hour (or overnight) before serving.

MINT CHOCOLATE CHIP ICE CREAM

🍴 SERVES: 4-6 🕐 PREP: 3 HRS 30 MINS 🕐 COOK: 0 MINS

INGREDIENTS:

- 14.5 oz full-fat coconut milk, infused with ¾ oz fresh mint sprigs*
- 3 egg yolks
- ½ cup creamed honey
- 1 tsp vanilla
- ⅛ tsp salt
- ⅓ cup chocolate chunks (see recipe from Chocolate Chip Cookie Cake, page 32)

*To infuse the coconut milk, bring milk to a boil in a small sauce pan. When milk is boiling, turn off heat and add fresh mint. Allow mint to steep until milk is cool, then transfer saucepan to fridge to continue steeping overnight.

METHOD:

1. Place egg yolks and honey in a medium mixing bowl and whisk until smooth. Set aside.

2. Remove saucepan from fridge and remove mint from milk. Squeeze mint into the saucepan to extract all liquid—this will ensure super mintiness!

3. Heat milk over medium heat in a small saucepan until just simmering.

4. Slowly pour hot milk into egg mixture, whisking constantly to temper eggs.

5. When all milk is whisked in, transfer mixture back to saucepan and return to low heat.

6. Continue whisking until mixture thickens into a custard-like consistency, about 15-20 minutes. Whisk in vanilla and salt.

7. Once mixture has thickened, remove from heat and pour into a small bowl or desired container. Allow mixture to cool completely, then transfer to fridge to chill 2 hours (or overnight).

8. Once mixture has cooled, pour into ice cream maker and process according to the instructions on the machine. Add chocolate chunks and stir to incorporate.

9. Transfer ice cream back to container and store in freezer. Allow it to freeze 1 hour (or overnight) before serving.

BANANA SPLIT ICE CREAM

SERVES: 6-8 **PREP: 3 HRS 30 MINS** **COOK: 0 MINS**

INGREDIENTS:

- 3 egg yolks
- ¾ cup mashed banana
- ¼ cup honey
- 14.5 oz can full-fat coconut milk
- 1 tbsp coconut oil
- 1 tsp vanilla
- ⅛ tsp salt
- 2 tsp lemon juice
- ¼ cup choc chunks
- ¼- ⅓ cup chopped toasted almonds
- ¼ - ⅓ cup finely minced strawberries

METHOD:

1. Place egg yolks, banana, and honey in a medium mixing bowl and whisk until smooth. Set aside.

2. Heat milk and oil over medium heat in a small saucepan until just simmering.

3. Slowly pour hot milk into egg mixture, whisking constantly to temper eggs.

4. When all milk is whisked in, transfer mixture back to saucepan and return to low heat.

5. Continue whisking until mixture thickens into a custard-like consistency, about 15-20 minutes. The mixture may seem thick at first, but continue heating and whisking it at least 15 minutes. Whisk in the vanilla, salt, and lemon juice.

6. When mixture is thickened, remove from heat and pour into a small bowl or desired container. Allow mixture to cool completely, then transfer to fridge to chill 2 hours (or overnight).

7. Once mixture has cooled, pour into ice cream maker and process according to the instructions on the machine.

8. Transfer ice cream back to container and stir in chocolate chunks, nuts, and strawberries.

9. Store in the freezer. Allow to freeze 1 hour (or overnight) before serving.

SALTED CHOCOLATE ICE CREAM WITH TOASTED ALMONDS & CACAO NIBS

SERVES: 4-6　　**PREP: 3 HRS 30 MINS**　　**COOK: 0 MINS**

INGREDIENTS:

- ¼ cup almonds, chopped
- 3 egg yolks
- 3-4 tbsp cacao powder (add more for a darker chocolate flavor)
- ½ tsp smoked sea salt
- ½ cup maple syrup
- 14.5 oz full-fat coconut milk
- 1 tsp vanilla
- ¼ cup cacao nibs OR chocolate chunks

METHOD:

1. Heat a small frying pan over medium heat. Add almonds and stir while they toast. When almonds are golden, transfer to a small bowl and set aside.

2. Place egg yolks, cacao, salt, and maple syrup in a medium mixing bowl and whisk until smooth. Set aside.

3. Heat coconut milk over medium heat in a small saucepan until just simmering.

4. Slowly pour hot milk into egg mixture, whisking constantly to temper eggs.

5. When all milk is whisked in, transfer mixture back to saucepan and return to low heat.

6. Continue whisking until mixture thickens into a custard-like consistency, about 15-20 minutes. Whisk in vanilla.

7. Once the mixture has thickened, remove from heat and pour into a small bowl or desired container. Allow mixture to cool completely, then transfer to fridge to chill 2 hours (or overnight).

8. Once the mixture has cooled, pour into ice cream maker and process according to instructions on the machine.

9. Transfer ice cream back to container and mix in almonds and chocolate chunks or cacao nibs.

10. Store in freezer. Allow to freeze 1 hour (or overnight) before serving.

SALTED CARAMEL ICE CREAM

SERVES: 4-6 **PREP: 3 HRS 30 MINS** **COOK: 0 MINS**

INGREDIENTS:

- 3 egg yolks
- ¼ cup ghee
- ½ cup coconut sugar
- 1 tbsp water
- 14.5 oz full-fat coconut milk
- 1-2 tsp vanilla extract
- ½ - ¾ tsp sea salt

METHOD:

1. Place egg yolks in a medium mixing bowl and whisk until smooth. Set aside.

2. In a medium saucepan heat ghee over medium heat. When ghee is melted, add sugar and water and stir to mix. Allow caramel to thicken, then slowly whisk in milk until smooth.

3. When mixture is completely combined, slowly pour warm caramel into egg yolks in a thin steady stream, whisking continuously to avoid clumping.

4. When all caramel is whisked in, transfer mixture back to saucepan and return it to low heat.

5. Continue whisking until mixture thickens into a custard-like consistency, about 15-20 minutes. Whisk in vanilla and salt.

6. Once mixture has thickened, remove from heat and pour into a small bowl or desired container. Allow mixture to cool completely, then transfer to fridge to chill 2 hours (or overnight).

7. Once mixture has cooled, pour into ice cream maker and process according to instructions on the machine.

8. Transfer ice cream back to container and store in freezer. Allow to freeze 1 hour (or overnight) before serving.

BALSAMIC ROASTED STRAWBERRY ICE CREAM

SERVES: 4-6   **PREP: 3 HRS 40 MINS**   **COOK: 50 MINS**

INGREDIENTS:

- 1 tbsp olive oil
- 2 tbsp maple syrup
- 1 tbsp balsamic vinegar
- 1 lb fresh strawberries
- 3 egg yolks
- ½ cup honey
- 14.5 oz full-fat coconut milk
- 1 tsp vanilla
- ⅛ tsp salt

METHOD:

Prepare the strawberries:

1. Preheat oven to 350°F. Line a baking sheet with parchment paper and set aside.
2. In a small bowl whisk together olive oil, maple syrup, and balsamic vinegar. Set aside.
3. Hull and chop strawberries into halves or quarters, depending on how large they are, and transfer them to a medium bowl.
4. Pour maple balsamic mixture over chopped berries and toss to make sure all berries are coated. Arrange berries in a single layer on prepared baking sheet, reserving balsamic mixture.
5. Roast berries until juices thicken but don't quite burn, about 45-50 minutes.
6. When berries are ready, remove from oven and transfer to a small bowl.
7. Mash roasted berries and 1 tablespoon of reserved balsamic mixture, and allow to cool completely before adding to ice cream.

Prepare the ice cream:

1. Place egg yolks and honey in a medium mixing bowl and whisk until smooth. Set aside.
2. Heat milk over medium in a small saucepan until just simmering.
3. Slowly pour hot milk into egg mixture, whisking constantly to temper eggs.
4. When all milk is whisked in, transfer mixture back to saucepan and return to low heat.
5. Continue whisking until mixture thickens into a custard-like consistency, about 15-20 minutes. Whisk in vanilla and salt.
6. Once mixture has thickened, remove from heat and pour into a small bowl or desired container. Allow mixture to cool completely, then transfer to fridge to chill 2 hours (or overnight).
7. Once mixture has cooled, pour into ice cream maker and process according to instructions on the machine. Mix in mashed strawberries.
8. Transfer ice cream back to container and store in freezer. Allow to freeze 1 hour (or overnight) before serving.

LEMON CHIFFON ICE CREAM

🍴 SERVES: 4-6   🕐 PREP: 3 HRS 35 MINS   🕐 COOK: 0 MINS

INGREDIENTS:

- 3 egg yolks
- ⅓ cup lemon juice
- ½ cup honey
- 1 tbsp lemon zest
- 14.5 oz can full-fat coconut milk
- 1 tsp vanilla
- 3 grams of stevia
- ⅛ tsp salt

METHOD:

1. Place egg yolks, lemon juice, and honey in a medium mixing bowl and whisk until smooth. Set aside.

2. Combine lemon zest with milk and heat mixture over medium in a small saucepan until just simmering. Allow mixture to simmer 3-5 minutes to infuse the milk.

3. Slowly pour hot milk into egg mixture, whisking constantly to temper eggs.

4. When all milk is whisked in, transfer mixture back to saucepan and return to low heat.

5. Continue whisking until mixture thickens into a custard-like consistency, about 20-25 minutes. This flavor takes a little longer to thicken because of added liquid from lemon juice. Whisk in vanilla, stevia, and salt.

6. Once mixture has thickened, remove from heat and pour into a small bowl or desired container. Allow mixture to cool completely, then transfer to fridge to chill 2 hours (or overnight).

7. Once mixture has cooled, pour into ice cream maker and process according to instructions on the machine.

8. Place ice cream back in its container and store in freezer. Allow to freeze 1 hour (or overnight) before serving.

S'MORES ICE CREAM

🍴 SERVES: 6   🕐 PREP: 3 HRS 40 MINS   🕐 COOK: 12 MINS

INGREDIENTS:

Graham Crumble

- 2 tbsp arrowroot
- 3 tbsp almond flour
- 1 tsp coconut flour
- 1 tbsp coconut oil
- 1 tbsp honey
- 1 tsp molasses
- ⅛ tsp salt

Ice Cream

- 3 egg yolks
- ½ cup maple syrup
- 14.5 oz full-fat coconut milk
- 1½ tsp vanilla
- ⅛ tsp salt
- ¼ cup chocolate chunks

METHOD:

Prepare the graham crumbles:

1. Preheat the oven to 350°F.
2. Combine all ingredients in a medium bowl and mix to form a dough.
3. Roll out dough between 2 pieces of parchment paper until dough is ¼-inch thick.
4. Remove one sheet of parchment paper and transfer rolled dough onto baking sheet, leaving it on the remaining piece of parchment paper.
5. Bake 10-12 minutes, until graham cracker is browned on the edges.
6. Remove from oven and transfer to a wire cooling rack. Allow graham cracker to cool completely before breaking it up into small pieces.

Prepare the ice cream:

1. Place egg yolks and maple syrup in a medium mixing bowl and whisk until smooth. Set aside.
2. Heat milk over medium in a small saucepan until just simmering.
3. Slowly pour hot milk into egg mixture, whisking constantly to temper eggs.
4. When all milk is whisked in, transfer mixture back to saucepan and return to low heat.
5. Continue whisking until mixture thickens into a custard-like consistency, about 15-20 minutes. Whisk in vanilla and salt.
6. Once mixture has thickened, remove it from heat and pour into a small bowl or desired container. Allow mixture to cool completely, then transfer to fridge to chill 2 hours (or overnight).
7. Once mixture has cooled, pour into ice cream maker and process according to instructions on the machine.
8. Transfer ice cream back to container and mix in chocolate chunks and graham cracker pieces.
9. Store ice cream in freezer. Allow it to freeze 1 hour (or overnight) before serving.

NO-CHURN AVOCADO ICE CREAM

🍴 SERVES: 4-6   🕐 PREP: 4 HRS 15 MINS   🕐 COOK: 0 MINS

INGREDIENTS:

- 1½ large avocados, ripe and soft
- ½ cup honey
- 2 cups coconut cream
- 2 tbsp lemon juice or lime juice
- ¼ tsp salt

METHOD:

1. Combine all ingredients in a blender and mix until smooth and creamy.

2. Pour mixture into a loaf pan or other container and freeze 4 hours (or overnight).

3. Allow ice cream to set out 5-10 minutes to soften before serving.